Welcome

The appeal of the Convair B-36 strategic bomber is timeless, not for any outstanding operational performance but rather for its statistics – sheer size, weight-lifting capacity, and intercontinental range. Flawed, yet historically important for the role it performed, transitional in that it was the last piston-engine bomber in service with the US Air Force and transformational, its ultimate guise combining both piston and jet engines on the same airframe, the 10-engine behemoth is referred to by some, affectionately and with ire, as the steam-punk bomber of the early Cold War years.

Conceived in the darkest hours of World War Two, when political leaders in Washington DC came to terms with the possibility of fighting Nazi Germany from US soil, the B-36 was a further manifestation of the Very Long Range bomber first realised in the Boeing B-29. With a specification requiring it to hit targets at extreme distance, the specification for the B-36 was unlike anything prepared before and it challenged airframe manufacturers and

engine builders to create the largest combat aircraft of its generation.

In this special publication we look at the early years of its design, the challenges faced in meeting initial and modified requirements, the competition seen off, and the complex problems in its development met head-on. Underpowered and slow, irksome to operate, and exposed to demanding environmental and operational requirements, the B-36 met and overcame many obstacles to point the way toward a truly hemispheric air force and future possibilities.

As well as looking at the aircraft itself, we will examine the arena it was created for, the early years of Strategic Air Command (SAC), and the operational demands placed on this nascent force, at the problems faced by integration with early atomic and thermonuclear bombs and by the new age of Cold War air power.

Throughout its relatively short service life the B-36 adapted to integration with existing types such as the B-29 and the B-50, improved in performance and flexibility, adopting a major role in reconnaissance and surveillance operations. Capable of

carrying every type of bomb in the US inventory and deployed with the largest aerial cameras carried by any aircraft, it served first as a test-bed for new equipment and advancing technology and then for experimental projects. In time it would play the role of carrier-plane to fighter-bombers, piggy-backing to hostile airspace, and as test equipment for a nuclear-powered engine.

The B-36 never dropped a bomb or fired its guns in anger, but in its 10-year operational life it provided solutions to a transformational way of waging war, being considered as a tool for a pre-emptive attack on the Soviet Union in a preventative first-strike which fortunately never happened. It served through the period when Russia acquired its own atomic bomb, and we examine the challenges posed as tensions increased and Strategic Air Command faced down a potential enemy with a global agenda. Welcome to the Convair B-36, the last Cold War bomber with piston-power.

David Baker
Editor

*COVER ARTWORK BY
ANTONIS KARIDIS*

BELOW: *The B-36
represented the dawn
of a new era in strategic
bombing with high
altitude, long range,
pressurised crew
compartments and both
nuclear and conventional
bomb loads. USAF*

Contents

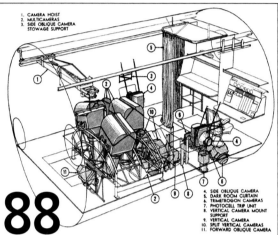

1. CAMERA HOIST
2. MULTICAMERAS
3. SIDE OBLIQUE CAMERA STOWAGE SUPPORT

4. SIDE OBLIQUE CAMERA
5. DARK ROOM CURTAIN
6. TRIMETROGON CAMERAS
7. PHOTOCELL TRIP UNIT
8. VERTICAL CAMERA MOUNT SUPPORT
9. VERTICAL CAMERA
10. SPLIT VERTICAL CAMERAS
11. FORWARD OBLIQUE CAMERA

Design: SJmagic DESIGN SERVICES, India
Advertising Sales Manager: Sam Clark
Email: sam.clark@keypublishing.com
Tel: 01780 755131
Advertising Production: Becky Antoniades
Email: Rebecca.antoniades@keypublishing.com

SUBSCRIPTION/MAIL ORDER
Key Publishing Ltd, PO Box 300, Stamford, Lincs, PE9 1NA
Tel: 01780 480404
Subscriptions email: subs@keypublishing.com
Mail Order email: orders@keypublishing.com
Website: www.keypublishing.com/shop

PUBLISHING
Group CEO and Publisher: Adrian Cox

Published by
Key Publishing Ltd, PO Box 100, Stamford, Lincs, PE9 1XQ
Tel: 01780 755131
Website: www.keypublishing.com

PRINTING
Precision Colour Printing Ltd, Haldane, Halesfield 1, Telford, Shropshire. TF7 4QQ

DISTRIBUTION
Seymour Distribution Ltd, 2 Poultry Avenue, London, EC1A 9PU
Enquiries Line: 02074 294000.

We are unable to guarantee the bona fides of any of our advertisers. Readers are strongly recommended to take their own precautions before parting with any information or item of value, including, but not limited to money, manuscripts, photographs, or personal information in response to any advertisements within this publication.

KEY Publishing

The Birth of the Big Bomber

Big bombers and new weapons reshape strategic air power.

Long before the first bombing raids were to shake civilians in their homes and 15 years before the start of World War One, in 1899 a group of international policy-shapers from several countries met at The Hague to discuss the fearsome prospect of attack from the air. Count von Zeppelin was already building his own rigid, lighter-than-air dirigibles, and the prospect of dropping explosives on troop concentrations and munitions dumps was foreseen as a plausible

reality. Not that it was Zeppelin's airships that brought fear and anxiety to this august gathering – there was far from any immediate probability of that – but the company had just registered its patent in the United States and that frightened many who previously had believed the country was protected by two great oceans.

The motion had been brought in a circular note from the Russians the previous year and at this First Hague Conference it was accepted, the

prohibition being confirmed again at the Hague IV conference on October 18, 1907, which under Article 25 asserted that "The attack or bombardment by whatever means, of towns, villages, dwellings or buildings which are undefended is prohibited". It was to remain in force until the third conference which has still to take place, in effect leaving it as a ratified agreement today.

The fearful prospect of unrestricted aerial bombardment was illuminated in H G Wells' classic tale, *The War in*

BELOW: *The Boeing XB-15, a late 1930s attempt to produce a long-range bomber for the US Army Air Corps but which was unsuccessful. USAAC*

RIGHT: *The First International Peace Conference in The Hague during 1899 decided to outlaw aerial bombardment of all non-military targets, four years before the Wright Brothers made the first powered flight and 15 years before World War One and the birth of air power.* Author collection

BELOW: *Germany made the first use of air power to bomb the strategic resources of another country, the Gotha G.V being used mainly for night attacks.* Author archive

the Air, published in 1908. In this fiction the Germans were the antagonists in an environment in which British and European aviation was about to evolve and the first aircraft to cross the English Channel landed in England in 1909 when the French aviator Louis Bleriot put his monoplane down on a grassy strip atop the cliffs near Dover. The modern British intelligence services

were formed and within five years the war which Wells foretold had erupted across continental Europe.

By 1918, Britain's Independent Force, which followed the amalgamation of the Royal Flying Corps and the Royal Naval Air Service into the Royal Air Force, demonstrated the strategic effect of bombing. Henceforth industrial, political and utilities supplying homes with light and

heat were considered legitimate military targets. Quickly upon its heels came the use of aerial bombardment to turn citizenry against its leadership, strategic bombing being the use of air power against the full spectrum of a nation's industrial might, including its work force. The edicts from Hague IV, it seemed, had been superseded by a new technology and very different ways of waging war.

Startfertigmachen eines deutschen Großflugzeuges
Einhängen der Bomben

Although the origin of strategic bombing is found in the role played by the Independent Force and the German airship and aircraft raids of World War One, it was lacking in the air power of the Luftwaffe 20 years later. Defined by some as strategic bombing, the use of air power during the second half of the 1930s supported attacks on mainland China and by the Luftwaffe against towns and cities in Spain during the war between nationalists and republicans, where the armed conflict became a testing ground for a new generation of weapons. But that definition is problematic. Strictly regarded as terror-bombing, these raids are sometimes referred to as strategic bombing but that is not so as they did little to diminish the strategic resources of the enemy.

Long debated among air historians, Germany's lack of a strategic air force was the result of a commitment to a 'blitzkrieg' strategy which aimed to use speed and firepower to overwhelm the enemy, first on the ground and in the air. Only then, over time, to use the navy to strike at the strategic assets of an enemy country by cutting off its imports and destroying its ability to protect merchant fleets by the use of surface and subsurface warships. In this way, only the navy was employed to strike strategic targets and only indirectly at that, the aircraft equipping the Luftwaffe for attack being designed for strikes at targets ahead of the front line and to prepare the battle space for advancing ground forces.

Only after its failure to destroy RAF Fighter Command was the Luftwaffe turned to attack strategic assets and targets directly related to munition production, imports, and manufacturing. It had neither the aircraft nor the strategy to make that effective and changes to procurement in favour of expanded fighter production, and a fully and effective air defence system using Chain Home radar stations, tipped the Battle of Britain to a war of attrition which the Luftwaffe lost, leaving the navy to press along with its

strategic role. One which would endure for the duration of the war, arguably the longest campaign in the history of World War Two.

However, only a year before Hitler came to power in 1933, Prime Minister Stanley Baldwin proclaimed that "the bomber will always get through", a phrase which could be taken as a cynical contempt for fighter advocates or a supportive endorsement of the bomber fraternity! Either way, Britain addressed the under-performing state of extant bombers through a development programme which would attempt to redress the balance, and formed RAF Bomber Command on July 14, 1936, along with Fighter Command, Coastal Command, and Transport Command in the same year.

Hard Learned Lessons

Gearing up for war, Britain was doomed to enter the conflict in September 1939 with light bombers such as the Bristol Blenheim and the Fairey Battle, medium bombers such as the Handley Page Hampden and the Vickers Wellington medium-range night bomber.

The decision made by the British government under Baldwin, and later followed by Neville Chamberlain, to focus national scientific and engineering resources on development of defensive weapons delayed the introduction of an offensive, strategic capability.

Considerable debate ensued behind closed doors around the benefits between offensive and defensive strategies, with atomic weapons and rockets for attack set against radar and anti-aircraft artillery for protection. It was the latter that won out, giving the Americans the lead in atomic weapons, and leaving rocketry well alone, despite a steady stream of intelligence to MI6 about German work in that sector during the late 1930s. And it was knowledge about German developments with radar, which

began in that country before World War One that supported plans for development of a fully operational Chain Home system.

While anticipating the introduction of the four-engine heavies, the Short Stirling and the Handley Page Halifax, the Avro Lancaster would meet the definitive longer-term requirements of Bomber Command, itself an outgrowth of the inadequately powered two-engine Manchester. Not before 1942-43 would the RAF be capable of putting up a strong and significantly effective strategic bomber force. By this time, the Americans were in the war, with Europe given priority, the Combined Bomber Offensive (CBO) beginning during the second half of 1942 but only reaching maturity more than a year later. It was the culmination of a policy struggle that began in April 1917.

For several years, the Americans had been studying air power policy and strategies for the use of aircraft in tactical and strategic duties and when they went to war in Europe, they took with them a comprehensive understanding of how the fighting powers had developed aerial warfare in both defensive and strategic roles. Advocates of strategic bombing included William 'Billy' Mitchell and Benjamin D Foulois who saw the aeroplane as an instrument for degrading the ability of a nation to wage war by destroying its infrastructure. Opposed, General William Pershing wanted to use air power in a purely tactical role and saw the aircraft much as the Germans

would see it when they reconstituted their air force in the 1930s.

The debate went on after the armistice of November 1918 and in the following years Mitchell worked tirelessly and at much personal cost to his reputation, refuting the claims by the US Navy that their warships were largely impervious to aerial bombardment. Conducted after the US Navy abolished its naval aviation arm, mixed results were returned from US Army trials conducted between 1921 and 1923 against old, retired warships in which bombers did prove conclusively that they could put bombs directly on to naval targets at sea. Not long afterwards, the US Navy turned again to aviation after which it never again withdrew support.

By the early 1930s, several different all-metal monoplane bombers were competing with each other and the subsidy of trans-continental

mail-carrying aircraft, together with the development of trans-Pacific flying boats sponsored the technology for fast, long-range bombers, typified by the Boeing 299 – the famous B-17. This aircraft was designed to a concept of self-defence in the belief that single-engine fighters could never be expected to escort long-range bombers all the way to their targets and back. Bristling with machine guns, the B-17 Flying Fortress was used by the Army Air Corps on very long range flights across the uncontested skies of Central and South America to demonstrate its performance and boast its capabilities.

When America entered World War Two, opposition to the CBO came from a difference of opinion on the way to employ the bombers: the British wanted large scale bombing of cities to destroy the factories and the homes of

LEFT: *The capacity of the B-29 to carry a wide range of bomb types sized the requirement for a very long-range strategic bomber and set the specification which grew with the B-36 design.*
Boeing

industrial workers while the Americans sought to pursue pin-point bombing of critical targets, factories, and unique facilities. The debate harked back to a study of strategic bombardment at the Air Corps Tactical School in 1930 where textbooks called for the development of specialised bomb-aiming equipment. That resulted in the Norden and Sperry bombsights and the development of those items preceded the arrival of the B-17 in the European theatre so that when operations began from England in 1942 the US Army Air Corps had distinctly superior bomb aiming equipment.

Carrying a crew of eight, the initial XB-17 had four defensive machine gun positions and a bomb carrying capacity of up to 4,800lb (2,177kg). With four Pratt & Whitney S1EG Hornet engines it boasted a top speed of 236mph (380kph) and a range of 3,100 miles (4,988km). It was the B-17E which would enter the fray from US Eighth Air Force bases in the UK during the second half of 1942. With four Wright R-1820-65 engines it had a maximum speed of 317mph (510kph), a cruising speed of 224mph (360kph) and a range of 2,000 miles (3,218kph) carrying a 4,000lb (1,814kg) bomb load.

The B-17E carried nine machine guns and the addition of a ball turret in the under-fuselage position; but the B-17G was the definitive development, 8,670 being manufactured by Boeing, Vega, and Douglas. Incorporating a new nose turret tested on the B-17F, the G had up to 13 machine guns and a maximum bomb load of 9,600lb (4,354kg). Of course, the maximum bomb load compromised range, and the assumption that the B-17 would be capable of defending itself proved flawed, driving a pause on the strategic bomber offensive for a redefinition of tactics more akin to that followed by

the RAF. The need for escort fighters pushed development of long-range versions of the P-47 and the P-51 but Luftwaffe pilots found the hail of fire from the bomber formations a formidable obstacle.

Speeding Up The Build

Historically, the US Amy had procured its aircraft through a process of research, design, development, and engineering followed by production. An orderly, systematic, and predictable cycle to which the US aviation industry had worked for several decades. Because of limitations in fast-track development and manufacture, the US Army compressed this conventional acquisition cycle into what became known as concurrency. The B-24, B-26, and B-29 were the first project types to adopt this flow path, which entered production much earlier in the development stage. This resulted in detailed design locking in certain vulnerabilities which could have catastrophic results.

For instance, the B-26 entered production with a wing too small to prevent five of the first six aircraft crashing due to a high stall speed. Only 'concurrent' modifications and redesign while the type was entering service partially solved what was always a tricky aircraft to fly. But the army wanted aircraft, quickly, and some degree of risk was accepted, the price for concurrency. Risks adopted by concurrency with relatively conventional aircraft did not bode well for sophisticated requirements, advanced design, and unusual specifications. Technologically ambitious, the B-29 originated as a pressurised version of the B-17 and with a tricycle undercarriage, resulting from a general desire to refine that type and expand its already considerable capabilities.

There was no particular US Army requirement or specification for Boeing to work to (although there soon would be) and design had begun on the Model 334 in March 1938 with high altitude capability built in. Refinements produced a development design in July 1939 and, as the Model 334B, this converged with a defined requirement from the army in January 1940. It wanted a 'super-bomber' capable of carrying a 2,000lb (907kg) bombload half way along a range of 5,333 miles (8,581km) at a speed of 400mph (644kph). This resulted in the Model 345 which was briefed to the US Army on May 11, 1940.

In January 1942, the month after America entered the war, an initial order for 250 from Boeing's Plant 2 at Wichita, Kansas, was increased to 500, production also assigned to Bell at Marietta, Georgia, North American at Kansas City, Kansas, and the Fisher Body Division of General Motors at Cleveland, Ohio. This was the first time such a large order had been placed for an aircraft which had not yet been built! The B-29 was no longer a pressurised, tricycle version of the B-17, having evolved into a very different aircraft shaped around requirements defined now by the prospect of American involvement in a European war.

The B-29 is important in the story of the B-36, introducing new features which would be standard on the latter. These included the pressurised cabin, remote-control gun turrets, new engines and propellers, and a requirement for high altitude flight in addition to the installation of precision bomb aiming

BELOW: *As an electronic tachometer, in the hands of an experienced bombardier the Norden bombsight provided great accuracy but was prone to drift in the gyroscope.*
Author archive

equipment. It too was fast-tracked through the concurrency approach. The technical challenges with this aircraft, heavier than anything built before, were greater than with any previous type, the wing loading being higher than previous types.

The wing loading of a B-17 came in at around 42lb/ft^2 (205kg/m^2) whereas the B-29 carried 69lb/ft^2 (337kg/m^2) and engineers at the Army Air Force (AAF) pressured Boeing to increase the wing area and reduce the load. Boeing was convinced that this would cut range and speed and incorporated Fowler flaps instead, which increased the wing area by 20% and also increased its lift coefficient.

Boeing did consider manned turrets such as those fitted to the B-17E, but they were rejected due to the extreme altitude at which the B-29 would operate, which was also the reason why it provided a shirtsleeve environment for the crew, fore and aft compartments being connected by a tunnel across the top of the unpressurised bomb bay. With two 0.5in machine guns and a 20mm cannon, the tail gunner would not have access to the pressurised compartments and would enter and exit at low altitude. These were learned lessons applied to the B-36, but also in remote-operation of the gun barbettes.

Two remote-control turrets were carried on the top of the fuselage and two below, controlled by a primary or secondary station. As designed, the B-29 had two bomb bays rather than the conventional single bay, with bomb release synchronised between the two with an intervalometer to prevent pitching moments. This would give the aircraft a greater flexibility in war load and in the adaptability for dividing bays for bombs or for supplementary fuel tanks, should that be necessary.

An important part of the design was the priority for a much cleaner wetted area than its predecessors, which for all its size had roughly the same drag as the B-17. This was helped by the suppressed profile of the gun barbettes

and the exterior design of the fuselage, which had few protuberances, and by the use of flush rivets which were a great improvement over the B-17. Another key feature of the B-29 was that with the exception of the nose wheel brakes, hydraulically operated control surfaces, bomb bay doors, and landing gear were fitted with electrically powered units, saving weight.

Self-evidently, the big bomber had arrived and production plans for the sustained delivery of the B-29 Superfortress obviated the need for an immediate successor. Had the war gone on into 1946 that might have been the case but when the Japanese sued for peace through intermediaries and the conflict ended before an Allied invasion of the Japanese mainland, it became apparent that the type would be just one more casualty of the 'peace dividend'. But shadowing the development of the B-29 was an even bigger bomber to dwarf its dimensions, a new aircraft incorporating much that had been trialled through the Superfortress and developed with learned lessons of combat experience. Ironically, a type which would never be used in anger.

Genesis of a Giant

Forged in wartime, the B-36 emerges after a competition for the world's biggest bomber.

The end of World War Two brought the cancellation of orders for 5,092 B-29s which would have been produced at the four manufacturing and assembly plants, the last of the 3,627 built being delivered on June 10, 1946. Of that total, 87 were supplied to the UK for operation by the RAF as the Washington B.1, the first arriving in March 1950 for service with 149 Squadron at Marham as a stop-gap between the Avro Lincoln and the English Electric Canberra. Other squadrons operating the type included Nos 15, 35, 44, 57, 115, and 207. Most of these aircraft had been retired out by 1954, a handful remaining with 90 Group for a further four years. Two Washington bombers had been transferred to the Royal Australian Air Force's Aircraft Research and Development Unit for trials organised by the Ministry of Supply, but they were scrapped in 1957.

The US aviation industry had seen rapid expansion and unprecedented production levels. Between July 1940 and August 1945 US armed services received 293,959 aircraft of which 158,880 (54%) went to the Army Air Forces. Deliveries to the AAF began slowly at first, with 8,723 in calendar year 1941 reaching a maximum of 51,547 in 1944 prior to a monthly decline through 1945. Of those totals, 27,867 Medium Bombers (B-17 and B-24) were delivered to the AAF in addition to 3,370 Very Heavy Bombers (B-29) in a classification which would quickly see those categories move down a notch, to Medium Bombers and Heavy Bombers, respectively. In terms of categories, heavy bombers accounted for 2% of deliveries in 1941, 19% in 1943 and 29% in 1944.

US Army Air Forces dropped a total 2,057,244 tons (1,866,332 tonnes) of bombs during World War Two, 75.5% in support of the defeat of Nazi Germany and the rest on Imperial Japan. The highest tonnage of bombs dropped in a single month was March 1945 with 200,211 tons (181,631 tonnes), 79.5% of which was dropped in the war against Germany. The highest tonnage in a single month against Japan was in July 1945 when 53,665 tons (48,685 tonnes) were dropped, of which 80% were delivered by the 20th Air Force.

At the end of World War Two, the AAF had 63,715 aircraft on strength, down considerably from the peak of 79,660 in July 1944, of which 11,065 were Heavy Bombers and 2,863 were Very Heavy Bombers (B-29s). In all, the B-17s, B-24s, and B-29s (13,928) represented 17.4% of the total AAF inventory. The total bomber inventory had increased markedly over the last 12 months of the war due to the expanded production of the B-29, increasing from 564 in August 1944 to 2,863 a year later. The AAF lost a total of 65,124 aircraft during the war, 43,581 of them overseas. Of these, 15,053 were bombers, of which 12,803 were lost on overseas deployments

In his summary of total air operations throughout the war in both theatres,

BELOW: *When introduced in the late 1940s, the B-36 was the largest US aircraft to enter production and posed major challenges in development. USAF*

General Arnold had some poignant observations which would be highly relevant for the post-war US Air Force:

"Although we were unprepared as a nation, we still had the time so essential to build a military force, time given us by our Allies fighting with their backs to the wall and by the distance of oceans. That precious time without doubt will not be given us again. Today, many modern war devices of great destructive power can be built piecemeal and under cover. Subassemblies might be secretly made in underground laboratories and assembled into an annihilating war machine. War may descend upon us by thousands of robots passing unannounced across our shorelines – unless we act now to prevent them."

The almost parallel genesis of the B-29 and the B-36 is emblematic of a time when several specifications were written in rapid succession for aircraft relatively close in sequential development, but each significantly enhanced in performance. The sequence of events leading to the B-36 requirement began contemporaneously with the origin of the B-29 and with that a new engineering challenge for the industry which would benefit the future development of the successor to the Superfortress.

Origins of a Concept

Although Boeing had a head start with a completely new successor to the B-17, the requirement in the US Army Air Corps (USAAC) originated a couple of years earlier via a special investigative committee set up by General Henry H Arnold, then head of the USAAC, and chaired by Brigadier General W G Kilner. It was tasked with determining the requirements of the air corps over the next several years and was influenced by testimony from Charles

Lindbergh following tours of German aircraft factories in 1936 and 1938. The initial report dated June 1939 had recommended development of an entirely new class of aircraft, a Very Long Range (VLR) bomber which would be capable of matching the specification to which Boeing had originally pegged the Model 334. That specification was upgraded in January 1940 in light of the German attack on Poland and it was to this requirement that the Boeing design goal was paired. But it was required to go through competitive tender.

Incorporating improved protective armour, self-sealing fuel tanks, greatly increased defensive armament and several refinements to the original specification, a Request for Data R-40B and Specification XC-218 was issued by the War Department on January 29, 1940. In addition to Boeing, it was circulated to Consolidated, Douglas, and Lockheed and on June 27, 1940, around the time France was finally falling to German forces, the USAAC issued contracts for engineering data with Boeing's bid designated XB-29, Lockheed's the XB-30, Douglas the XB-31, and Consolidated the XB-32.

Lockheed opted for a 12-man aircraft powered by 2,200hp Wright R-3350-13 air-cooled radial engines and with a pressurised compartment, but in starting late it perceived a technical disadvantage to Boeing and withdrew. Much of its initial work on the XB-30, however, went in to the L-049 Constellation for a design which originated prior to the bomber project and out of which the XB-30 concept had emerged. But converting a triple-fin airliner into a very long range bomber was never going to work.

Douglas designed their Model 423 contender into the largest of all four proposals, with four 28-cylinder Pratt & Whitney R-4360s each delivering 3,000hp. Displaying large tail fin and rudder, the XB-31 had a double-bubble cockpit with pilot and co-pilot seated separately and six crew members at individual stations throughout the aircraft. There never was a single Douglas contender which, like Lockheed, took so much of the design heritage from the DC-4. Airliners do not make good bombers!

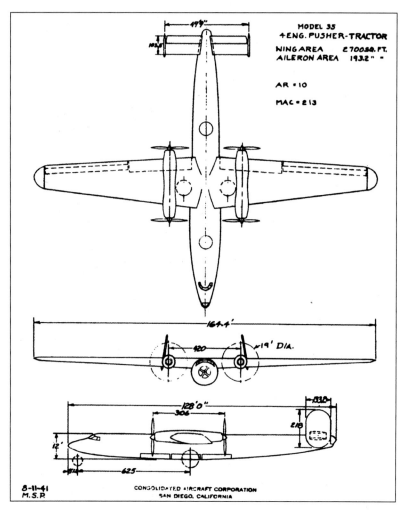

MODEL 35
4 ENG. PUSHER-TRACTOR

WING AREA   2700 SQ. FT.
AILERON AREA   193.2 " "

AR = 10

MAC = 213

8-11-41
M.S.P.

CONSOLIDATED AIRCRAFT CORPORATION
SAN DIEGO, CALIFORNIA

LEFT: *Initial concept drawing for the Consolidated Model 35 in response to the requirement for a Very Large Bomber issued on May 3, 1941.* Consolidated

bigger and more capable than the B-29 would be required.

This would be no normal competition. Constrained by high security, the Air Corps Materiel Division set minimum performance requirements at a range of 8,000 miles (12,872km), carrying a 4,000lb (1,814kg) bomb load at a maximum speed of 350mph (563kph). But it also had to be capable of supporting a 12,000 mile (19,308km) mission at 450mph (724kph) and an altitude of 45,000ft (13,716m). The optimum performance specified a 10,000lb (4,536kg) bomb load with a range of 10,000 miles (16,090km) dropping the war load half way and returning to base or proceeding on downrange to a friendly destination. They also stipulated a stressed design capable of carrying a maximum 72,000lb (32,659kg) bomb load over a reduced range, a cruising speed of 300-400mph (483-644kph) and the capability to operate off a 5,000ft (1,524m) runway.

To some engineers these requirements appeared outrageous. The B-17 had an affective combat radius of little more than 1,000 miles (1,609km) at best, while the B-29, still to fly, would reach targets 2,500 miles (4,022km) away. To a large degree it was a fishing exercise; even the Materiel Division was not at all sure that this performance was possible and, with uncharacteristic latitude, asked the contractors to examine "the aeronautical art and to determine what may be technically possible...within the next three or four years." This was an unusually

Consolidated had marginally better luck with their XB-32, the type being retained as a hedge against problems with the B-29. Similar to the highly successful B-24, initially the XB-32 had a twin-fin tail unit but that was replaced by a large dorsal fin and rudder. The aircraft was beset with numerous technical problems and design flaws which prevented it being deployed in the role for which it was designed. Only 15 entered service as the Convair B-32 Dominator from 1945.

In March 1943, Consolidated changed its name to Convair when it merged with Vultee Aircraft and was more formally known as Consolidated-Vultee. In that regard, the story of the B-32 also blends in to that of the B-36. Had the B-29 been less successful and the B-32 more prominent in the inventory of the US Army Air Forces, the story of the B-36 may have been very different. Nevertheless, Boeing got the job building the VLA as the B-29 Superfortress.

On April 11, 1941, when only a wooden mock-up of the B-29 existed and before prototype assembly had started, Boeing and Consolidated were each asked to submit proposals for an intercontinental bomber which would have the capacity to wage war on Nazi Germany from the US mainland. The idea had been developing since a meeting between

President Roosevelt and Army Chief of Staff General George C Marshall, together with US Army Air Corps leaders, determined that something

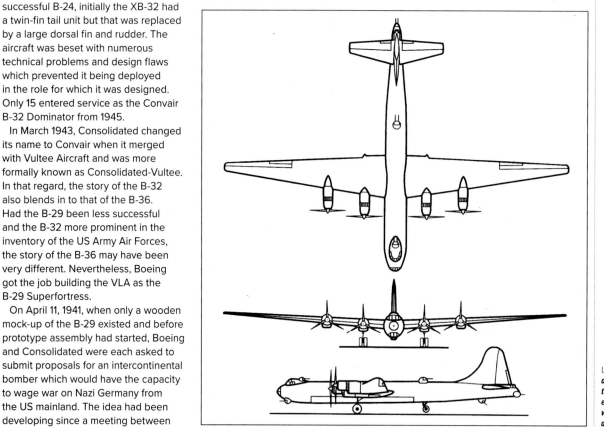

LEFT: *Boeing's Model 334 design was little more than a developed evolution of the B-29 with a similar engine arrangement.* Boeing

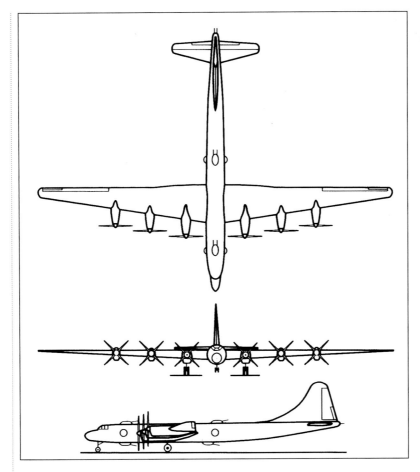

compensated with the balance. The Model 35 was larger than the B-29, the first prototype of which was then being assembled, but it was unimpressive and unable to meet the stipulated requirement, a problem also experienced by the other contenders.

Drop-Outs

Submitted on May 3, Boeing's Model 384, and its later 385, also failed to impress as they each appeared to be a lacklustre attempt at meeting a compromise position on range. The Model 384 had four engines with tractor propeller arrangements and looked to some extent like a stretched B-29; the Model 385 had six tractor engines with each design featuring defensive armament in two dorsal, two ventral, and single tail turrets. Unsurprisingly, the 385 had a high-aspect ratio wing very similar to the B-29.

Within several weeks of the initial request for concept designs, Northrop and Douglas became involved with Consolidated, Boeing and Douglas submitting design data for their individual concepts. Northrop had been keen to push its flying-wing concept and on May 27, 1941, Air Materiel Command requested further details but while it could satisfy the 10,000lb (4,536kg) bomb load the range was a poor 6,000 miles (9,654km) - far short of that required. Northrop's flying wing was a radical concept to minimise drag and improve aerodynamic efficiency by eliminating the need for tail planes, a conventional fuselage incorporating

loose definition of a requirement, more a request for advice by way of design concepts.

The air corps wanted to resist writing hard specifications until it had sound recommendations and was prepared to delay defining a particular requirement until it had suggestions from industry. Agreeing to come up with design proposals, the following month Boeing and Consolidated were joined by Northrop and Douglas. With early data from some wind tunnel research, the general configuration of such a behemoth was found plausible. The National Advisory Committee for Aeronautics (NACA) became involved and supported the industry studies with their own tests.

The first response was submitted by Consolidated on May 3, 1941, for its Model 35, equipped with four engines but twin fins and rudders, retaining the manufacturer's preference for the configuration adopted for the B-24. The Model 35 had a fuselage length of 128ft (39m), a wing span of 164.4ft (50.1m) with four engines in a paired pusher-tractor configuration on each inner wing extending 25.5ft (7.7m) between forward and aft propeller bosses. The twin fins spanned 49.75ft (15.1m). With tricycle undercarriage, the aircraft would have had a conventional cockpit layout, three bomb bays and unspecified defensive armament. But an aircraft with this range would have to fly without escort.

Consolidated had been working the large bomber concept for several months, its own money now supplemented by a fee of $435,523 divided between Consolidated and Boeing, the winner promised just over $300,000 and the loser being

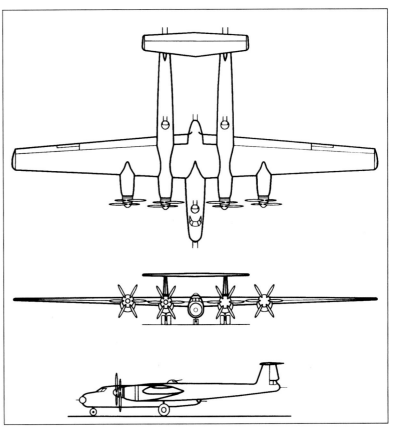

study was accompanied by a general arrangement drawing."

The proposal from Consolidated was sent to the AAF on October 6, 1941, along with a costing analysis and a request for $800,000 to assemble two prototypes. The company was aware of difficulties defined earlier under the fast-track, concurrency management concept and specifically asked that it be kept free of interference and continuous changes and revisions to the requirement. In fact, the B-36 would prove to be one of the most troubled, dysfunctional programmes of the period and continuously in a state of flux, demonstrably exhibited by its evolution long after production orders had been received. But it was not the proposal from Consolidated that had first excited the AAF. That would be the flying-wing concept from Northrop, about which more on page 44.

A key aspect of operations analysis with the B-29 during World War Two was to determine the value of defensive armament for future aircraft, some of which factored in to the B-36. With an impending generation of very large bombers, effective protection from attack was the key to mission success and survivability. The B-17 entered service bristling with machine guns

crew and bomb-carrying equipment within a blended wing centre-section.

Other manufacturers got involved, including North American Aviation which proposed a twin-boom layout, a single boom extending back from each inner pair of its four engines and a truncated fuselage emerging from the wing centre-section. Bomb bays were fitted to each tail boom assembly. Designated NA-116, this proposal had very little traction and disappeared from the list of contenders. Nor was the initial proposal from Douglas acceptable, their Model 423 design featuring the same range limitation as the Northrop flying wing. In fact, all four major studies got bogged down in the complexity of producing a workable design to meet the demanding specification.

Responding, officials and air staff leaders from the newly re-named Army Air Force (AAF) met on August 19 for a conference to discuss the study results and issue an amended specification, retaining the full range and bomb load but downgrading the speed requirement while setting a service ceiling of 40,000ft (12,192m). Defensive armament was to comprise six 37mm cannon and eight 0.50in machine guns to match the need to defend against attack from three fighters simultaneously. But this added weight to the aircraft and threatened a workable solution to the range problem. The meeting took place before Boeing received formal approval for its studies while Consolidated had still to complete its final investigation.

The four contractors were pressed to submit their proposals immediately and all were in the hands of the AAF by mid-September, at which point Douglas and Boeing dropped out, the former believing the specification asked the physically impossible. Perhaps through preoccupation with existing and pending contracts as the aviation and munitions

industry went into war-fever, none of the four contenders had provided proper studies to the satisfaction of the customer, the AAF declaring that "in no case was sufficient aerodynamic data submitted to permit a complete check" of the performance, "only one of the design studies contained data giving the amount of fuel carried, and only one

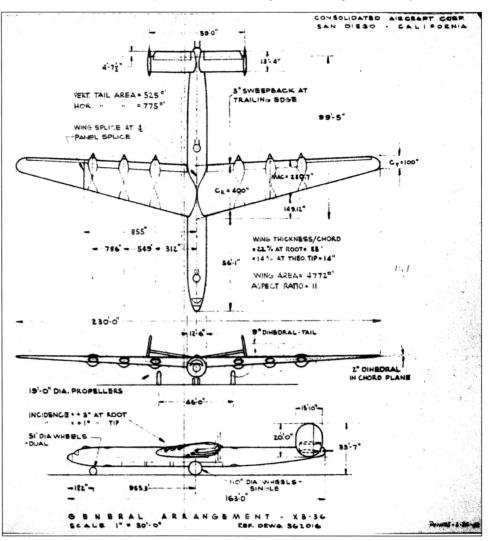

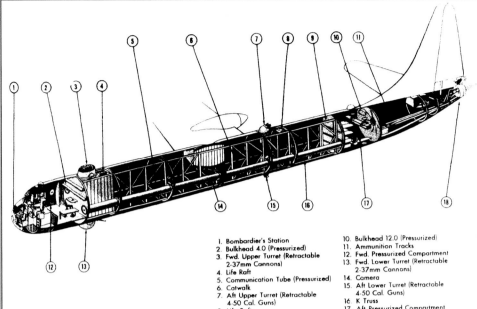

1. Bombardier's Station
2. Bulkhead 4.0 (Pressurized)
3. Fwd. Upper Turret (Retractable 2-37mm Cannons)
4. Life Raft
5. Communication Tube (Pressurized)
6. Catwalk
7. Aft Upper Turret (Retractable 4-50 Cal. Guns)
8. Life Raft
9. Bulkhead 10.0 (Pressurized)
10. Bulkhead 12.0 (Pressurized)
11. Ammunition Tracks
12. Fwd. Pressurized Compartment
13. Fwd. Lower Turret (Retractable 2-37mm Cannons)
14. Camera
15. Aft Lower Turret (Retractable 4-50 Cal. Guns)
16. K Truss
17. Aft Pressurized Compartment
18. Tail Turret (2-50 Cal. Guns & 1-37mm Cannon)

ABOVE: *Similar to the internal layout of the B-29, the B-36 had two pressurised sections fore and aft connected by a tunnel for crew movements between the two areas. USAF*

RIGHT: *Manufacturing such a large aircraft brought opportunities for innovative, weight-saving solutions including the bonding of separate panels by adhesives to provide a smoother wetted area, as seen here in Building 4 at Consolidated's Fort Worth facility. Consolidated*

BELOW: *On the ground and in the air, the extended tubular-shaped fuselage gave the B-36 a nickname of 'the cigar with wings'. USAF*

and cannons and that only increased as the type evolved through successive variants, culminating in the B-17G with its characteristic chin turret. Carried forward to the large bombers of the future, heavy defensive gun positions weighed against the aircraft's overall performance and cut into potential bomb-carrying loads.

Conclusions from a detailed analytical report on the effectiveness of B-29 defensive armament with XX Bomber Command which was submitted on February 10, 1945, indicated that under some circumstances there was little or no need for defensive positions. The survey found that the "gunnery system has been moderately effective against frontal attacks, whereas enemy attacks from this direction have been very effective." It found that it had been "least effective against side attacks, however enemy attacks from this direction have also been ineffective," and that the "gunnery system has been highly effective against rear attacks whereas rear attacks from enemy aircraft have been ineffective."

The statistical analysis showed that for every 100 encounters with fighters, B-29 losses would be 2.3 from frontal attacks, 0.4 from side attacks and 0.2 from the rear. However, enemy losses per 100 encounters stood at 7.8 when

attacking from the front, 6.3 from side attacks and 14.7 from rear attacks. It found that the ratio of enemy losses to B-29 losses per 100 encounters was 3.4 for frontal attacks, 14.8 for side engagements and 70.0 for attacks from the rear. The gunnery system on the B-29 was deemed one of the most effective developed to this date and proposed that attention should be focused on "improving and perfecting the present remote control turret system rather than to experimenting with alternate armament arrangements."

Interestingly, the report recommended that "serious consideration should be given to the use of stripped aircraft for daylight bombing, but only under the conditions that a wide angle tail turret be installed and that escort aircraft with flexible guns accompany the stripped aircraft for defense against frontal attacks." The results reported from enemy engagements with the Japanese army and navy air forces were compared with an extensive series of tests and training exercises which B-29 crews had gone through during development of air gunnery tactics at Alamogordo, New Mexico. There was a reassuringly strong correlation between the simulated engagements and the actual encounters during combat operations.

Refining the Design

Proposals and improvements to a design far from satisfactory and in dire need of modification.

On November 15, 1941 Consolidated received a contract to build two XB-36 aircraft. A week later the company engineers selected Model 36 as the optimum configuration, for which the type designation had been numerically aligned. Many late hours had been spent deliberating over the specifics of each concept, and a wide range of analyses had been conducted before the final iteration was selected. There was a palpable sense of impending production requirements following the attack by Germany on the Soviet Union five months earlier, and politicians were debating the consequences of a global expansion in the conflict.

Tensions with the empire of Japan had been increasing over the past few years, triggered by concerns over attacks on China and by demands on trade and maritime access which were contested by the Americans. Increasingly belligerent, the Tojo government sought to break a blockade imposed by the United States, who saw in their militaristic defiance a potential threat to interests in the Philippines. Nobody, however, really expected Japan to attack the United States directly when it struck at Pearl Harbor in an attempt to neutralise the Pacific Fleet which would threaten its race into Southeast Asia and eventually down as far south as Papua, New Guinea.

The need for a bomber of great range, capable of crossing vast swathes of intercontinental ocean was unique to the North and South American land mass, any credible enemy at greater distance than for any country other than the United States. Consequently, it was for range that the AAF sought a solution to the extended mission requirement through an aerodynamically clean airframe and a high-lift, high aspect-ratio wing The arrangement of fuselage, wing, tail and location of engines was driven by that and channelled Consolidated into buried engines with leading-edge air intakes and pusher propellers, six of which were placed in the aft wing sections which had a total span of 230ft (70.1m).

The design concept initially incorporated six Pratt & Whitney

ABOVE: *The enormous size of the B-36 (above) was evident from a staged photo-shoot at Carswell AFB displaying several generations of bomber from the B-18 Bolo (behind), the B-17 (foreground) and the B-29 (left). USAF*

X-Wasp, air-cooled radial engines each driving three-bladed propellers sweeping a diameter of 19ft (5.8m). The wing was set high on the cylindrical, cigar-like fuselage which had a length of 163ft (49.7m) supporting a horizontal tail with twin-fins giving the aircraft a height of 35.8ft (10.9m). The aircraft was designed to carry a load of 72,000lb (32,659kg), the bombs and ordnance contained in four separate bays, and with forward and aft pressurised crew compartments connected by a pressurised tube tunnel, 80ft (24.4m) in length and with a diameter of 25in (63.5cm) located above and to the port side of the bomb bays. With this, crewmembers could move fore or aft lying supine on a trolley using a rope, hand-over-hand, to pull themselves along.

Personal comfort was a key factor in the internal layout and provision for a large crew, members of which would serve in relays across what could be missions lasting up to two days in the air, included bunks, a galley, and a toilet in the aft pressurised section. These facilities would be improved over time and were initially designed in as reference points for different pieces of equipment as requirements demanded and crew numbers changed.

The initial design could not benefit from the later studies of B-29 defensive armament performance and consisted of five 37mm cannon and ten .50 calibre machines guns in four retractable turrets in dorsal and ventral positions together with a radar-controlled tail turret. Many changes would be made to this configuration as the type went

through successive variants, responses to changing technical requirements, and the inevitable compromises as detailed design and assembly ran in parallel. Initially, the Model 36 had a fuel capacity of 21,116 US gal (79,924 lit) in tanks integral to the wings. The cockpit had conventional side-by-side seating for pilot and co-pilot with engineer and navigator stations behind.

This was a big aircraft by any standard, and recognising the challenges that could pose for manufacturing and assembly it was in-service maintenance and servicing that received the highest level of attention. An aircraft of this size would be expensive to procure and costly to maintain. Any savings there would be identified as a positive step during assessment by the contracts board. Weight was a serious problem

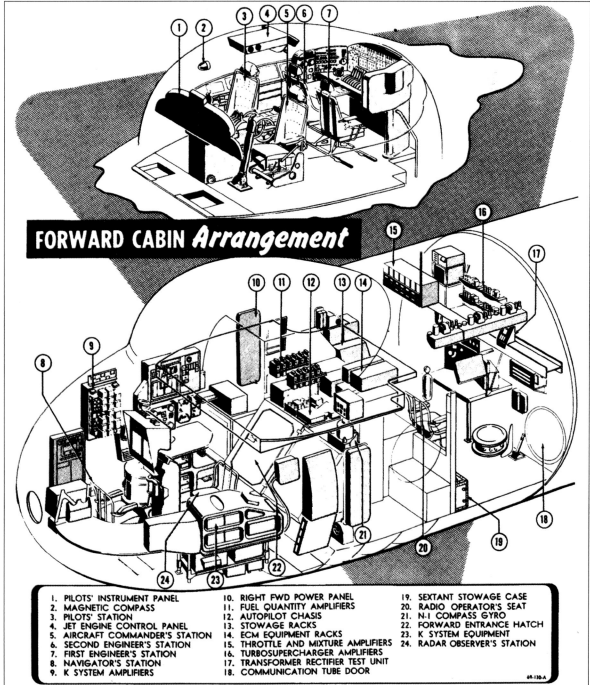

FORWARD CABIN *Arrangement*

1. PILOTS' INSTRUMENT PANEL	10. RIGHT FWD POWER PANEL	19. SEXTANT STOWAGE CASE
2. MAGNETIC COMPASS	11. FUEL QUANTITY AMPLIFIERS	20. RADIO OPERATOR'S SEAT
3. PILOTS' STATION	12. AUTOPILOT CHASIS	21. N-1 COMPASS GYRO
4. JET ENGINE CONTROL PANEL	13. STOWAGE RACKS	22. FORWARD ENTRANCE HATCH
5. AIRCRAFT COMMANDER'S STATION	14. ECM EQUIPMENT RACKS	23. K SYSTEM EQUIPMENT
6. SECOND ENGINEER'S STATION	15. THROTTLE AND MIXTURE AMPLIFIERS	24. RADAR OBSERVER'S STATION
7. FIRST ENGINEER'S STATION	16. TURBOSUPERCHARGER AMPLIFIERS	
8. NAVIGATOR'S STATION	17. TRANSFORMER RECTIFIER TEST UNIT	
9. K SYSTEM AMPLIFIERS	18. COMMUNICATION TUBE DOOR	

44-130-A

RIGHT: *Upper and lower decks for the forward pressurised compartment offered unprecedented access to crew positions including pilots, navigators, radio operators, engineers, and bombardier.* Convair

with this large aircraft and savings in manufacturing would bring dividends in range and payload capacity.

In an attempt to reduce drag from several thousand pop-rivets, the company conducted research on alternative methods of securing separate elements together, including the use of a special metal adhesive. Available in both liquid and tape, it was applied progressively throughout the construction of the aircraft to a greater number of structural elements until, by the early 1950s, almost one-third of the exterior surface was bonded using these forms.

But there was concern about the fatigue life of this new adhesive, and special tests were conducted, revealing a much better performance than mechanical fasteners. A spot-welded technique would complete 12 million cycles before failure compared with 18 million for riveted joins and 240 million cycles for the new metal-bonding adhesive. This was but one example of the way the programme provided opportunity for pioneering techniques and materials never used before, including new system concepts and engineering design.

A significant research effort resulted in a new means of satisfying the hydraulic and electrical requirement, driven in part by the large dimensions of the flying control surfaces. Believing that the standard AAF requirement for a 1,500psi (10,342kPa) hydraulic system was inadequate for moving the oversize undercarriage and the large flaps, Consolidated developed a 3,000psi (20,685kPa) system with the assistance of engineers from the AAF at Air Service Command, set up at Wright Field, Ohio, in March 1941. Everything associated with this new hydraulic system was functionally re-designed, and this would become the standard for all US military aircraft for several decades.

Wright Field developed the electrical system for the XB-36, where a new 400-cycle, 208 volt, three-phase alternating current (AC) system had been developed. This was adopted to

AIRPLANES NOT IN GROUP 6

1. COMMUNICATION TUBE DOOR
2. FIRE EXTINGUISHER
3. PRESSURE REGULATOR
4. BUNKS
5. UPPER RIGHT GUNNER'S STATION
6. TAIL GUNNER'S STATION
7. TAIL COMPARTMENT ENTRANCE
8. AFT CABIN ENTRANCE HATCH
9. GUNNERS' PLATFORM
10. UPPER LEFT GUNNER'S STATION
11. LOWER LEFT GUNNER'S STATION

AIRPLANES IN GROUP 6

1. COMMUNICATION TUBE DOOR
2. FIRE EXTINGUISHER
3. PRESSURE REGULATOR
4. BUNKS
5. STOWAGE RACK
6. DINING TABLE
7. LIQUID CONTAINERS *
8. UPPER RIGHT GUNNER'S STATION
9. PARACHUTE BAG RACK
10. TAIL GUNNER'S STATION
11. TAIL COMPARTMENT ENTRANCE HATCH
12. AFT ROOMETTE
13. ACCESS LADDER
14. AFT CABIN ENTRANCE HATCH
15. GUNNER'S PLATFORM
16. UPPER LEFT GUNNER'S STATION
17. GALLEY UNIT
18. LOWER AFT GUNNER'S STATION

CI-134-C

replace the direct current (DC) system used on other, and previous aircraft. The logic in this was found in weight saving alone, an AC system weighing less than one-quarter the weight of an equivalent DC system. Moreover, it was more reliable and less prone to breaking down and at high altitude was

less prone to arcing, another technology development which would become standard on US combat aircraft.

Fire extinguishing too benefitted from a switch to a methyl-bromide system replacing the standard carbon-dioxide suppressant usually installed within the engine casings. Moreover, it had a lower boiling point and that allowed safe containment at lower pressures in lighter cylinders. As a further example of the evolving nature of systems installation, this new fire extinguishing equipment was not ready for the first XB-36 prototype but would be incorporated in subsequent aircraft as well as the XC-99 (which we'll discuss later).

These developments were typical of the contributions made by the programme with its tightly compressed layers of detailed design, tests, engineering refinement, systems development and assembly, a seminal example of compressed concurrency with all the flaws and failures that this

ABOVE: Improvements to the crew quarters in the aft pressurised compartment introduced better facilities and upgraded equipment. Note the tail compartment entrance hatch. Convair

LEFT: Rest periods for relay crew were spasmodic with little respite from noise, frequent turbulence, and continuous activity from the operating stations. Via Dennis Jenkins

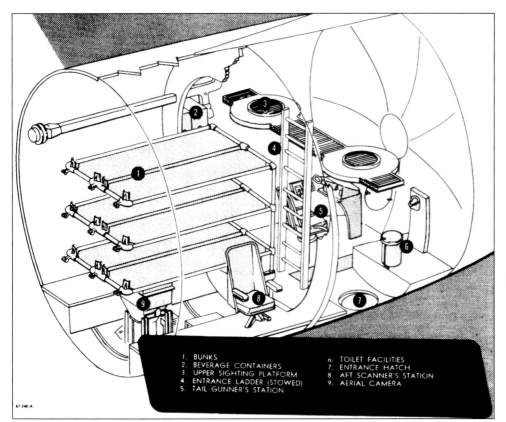

1. BUNKS
2. BEVERAGE CONTAINERS
3. UPPER SIGHTING PLATFORM
4. ENTRANCE LADDER (STOWED)
5. TAIL GUNNER'S STATION
6. TOILET FACILITIES
7. ENTRANCE HATCH
8. AFT SCANNER'S STATION
9. AERIAL CAMERA

67-240-A

ABOVE: *A typical bunk area, the configuration of which would change according to bomber or reconnaissance roles, the number of crewmembers and the equipment required. Convair*

incurred. But in projecting from the near-term to mid-term requirements, concurrency did stimulate new, sometimes radical, engineering solutions and as such it served as a technology pathfinder.

Reworking the Design
Consolidated leaned heavily on the wind tunnel facilities at the Massachusetts Institute of Technology (MIT) and at the Guggenheim Aeronautical Laboratory of the California Institute of Technology (GALCIT) where initial 1/26th scale models were used. Examining the abundant options available from NACA, Consolidated selected the NACA-65 profile which was a laminar-flow wing exhibiting high lift and low drag and offering limited wind resistance, for which the appendages were arranged for optimum performance. It didn't last long. In July 1942 Consolidated changed this to a NACA-63 profile with a modified trailing-edge forward sweep of 3° from the root to the tip which improved the centre of gravity and the balance.

One advantage for the company was its familiarity with building large aircraft, notably the amphibious PBY Catalina, the B-24 Liberator, and the P2BY Coronado flying boat which had been in service since December 1940. Not so familiar was its scaling up for large production runs, although the B-24 would quickly provide that, but its engineering heritage leaned on a distinguished line of training aircraft that the company had developed since being formed in Buffalo, New York,

during the early 1920s, a pedigree of lightweight types culminating in the two-seat, closed-cockpit, retractable landing gear P-30, the only such aircraft operated by the USAAC from 1935.

In a building near to its design and engineering offices and the San Diego manufacturing plant, Consolidated prepared a wooden mock-up which also served as a test rig for the exterior design and the defensive armament stations with the landing gear getting special attention due to the projected weight of the aircraft and the landing forces that would be imposed. Consolidated had manufacturing experience from the 18,188 B-24s built for US and Allied air forces, more than any other American combat aircraft. That programme had been managed by I M Laddon who had been the chief engineer on the Catalina and, as executive vice-president of Engineering, would play a seminal role in the B-36, with design and engineering managed by Harry A Sutton and Ted P Hall running the design group during the early phases.

On July 20, 1942, the mock-up review and projected performance figures were evaluated and revealed a deficiency in range, well short of the 10,000 miles (16,090km) specified, triggering a discussion about aerodynamic performance and drag-reduction steps which at one point considered removing some of the defensive armament and their protrusions from the wetted area. To have done so would have partially solved the problem, but under known

RIGHT: *Essential for extended flights on reconnaissance missions, the bunk arrangement was flexible and configured according to needs. Via Dennis Jenkins*

twin vertical tails, a characteristic of the B-24 but which would be changed to a single, vertical tail to avoid stress and overload during a hard landing. Similar concerns had persuaded Consolidated to give the B-32 a single-tail configuration, as did Boeing for the B-29, and the change order was signed off on October 10, 1943. It shaved 3,850lb (1,746kg) off the dry weight but brought a three-month delay in delivering the first XB-36 due to redesign and fabrication work at what was already a low-priority programme. But that would quickly change.

ABOVE: *A crewmember demonstrates the technique for using the access tunnel, a procedure best reserved for fine-weather flying!* Via Dennis Jenkins

LEFT: *Located along the lower port side of the fuselage, the access tunnel between fore and aft pressurised compartments afforded access in flight by way of a trolley and hand-over-hand rope.* Via Dennis Jenkins

characteristics of air combat scenarios, would have left the aircraft dangerously exposed to attack in contested airspace.

Meanwhile, in August the decision was made to move the programme to Fort Worth, Texas, and into Government Aircraft Plant No 4 about 1,200 miles (1,931km) east of San Diego. The move allowed expansion of the B-24 subassembly production lines, but Fort Worth also began to experience added work on B-24 production, followed by the B-32 Dominator from 1943.

The general expansion of aircraft production driven by the rearmament programme had a significant impact on the short-term needs of the army and early difficulties in the Pacific against Japan's Imperial Navy intensified the demand for aircraft already in the early production stage as well as for the B-29, which was significantly along in its development. All this argued against an acceleration of long-term projects such as the B-36, which was essentially put on hold so that available, flight-proven types could be granted priority on the production line. But it was not all bad news.

In mid-1942 the AAF agreed to a cargo version which would emerge as the XC-99 on the proviso that this would only appear at least three months after the first flight of the XB-36. Consolidated had wanted to fast-track the cargo version so that, unencumbered with the design and integration of defensive armament and combat kit, it could be used to prove out the general configuration and aerodynamic performance of the aircraft including engines and landing gear. Nevertheless, this was a false expectation because the basic design of the aircraft was still in a state of flux and

with considerable work still required to complete the prototypes.

After thorough inspection of the mock-up, the design was approved in September 1942 with the caveat that changes would be necessary with the

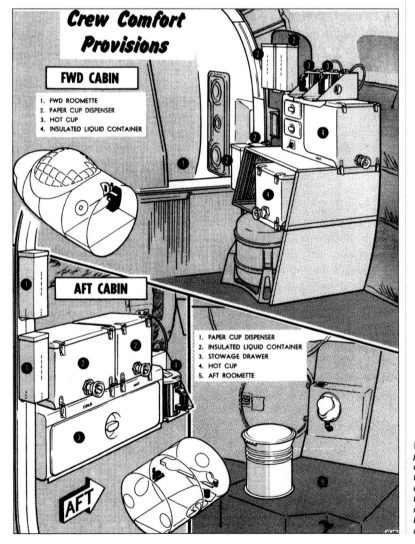

LEFT: *The forward pressurised section contained provisions for food preparation and cooking, essential for flights which could last more than 24 hours on long reconnaissance missions.* Convair

RIGHT: *The B-36 had potential for troop and cargo transport and would result in a parallel contract for the XC-99, the oversize fuselage providing upper and lower levels capable of accommodating up to 400 people.* Convair

At this period in the chronology, Consolidated changed its name to Convair in November 1942 when Vultee Aircraft Corporation bought a controlling interest, effectively marked up on its letterheads and advertising boards from March 17, 1943. But it was good times for the company. A letter of authorisation was received on July 23 ordering 100 B-36 aircraft through W33-038-ac-7 with a worth of $175m. There were those who nursed hopes that the B-36 could supplant the B-29 on wartime production lines as that aircraft continued to pose serious challenges, but this was never possible, and Boeing worked through its problems with support from the AAF.

But the B-36 had its own problems. Concern about the X-Wasp engine (see page 40) directed attention toward the in-line Lycoming BX which had a lower fuel consumption and offered increased range. Lycoming had also hoped that its 36-cylinder radial XR-7755 would be selected for the B-36. With nine banks of four-row cylinders and a rated output of 5,000hp (3,728kW), this engine would have had a specific fuel consumption of 0.485lb/hp-hr (0.295kg/kW-hr) at a throttle setting of 70%. It was clearly too late for major investment, the emerging generation of jet engines bringing an end to the development of new and increasingly powerful reciprocating engines. Convair was stuck with the X-Wasp, but that too was proving troublesome although there was concern that choosing to run in parallel with an alternative engine would add development to the basic aircraft.

BELOW: *The definitive nose configuration showing the glazed section for the forward armament and the bombardier's position with the upper level providing side-by-side seating for the pilots.* USAF

Price and Pace

The cost of a B-36 was going to be three times that of a B-29 and parallel development of the two aircraft would never have been possible in peacetime.

The air staff and the leadership of the AAF balanced needs and requirements against wants and possibilities, the B-29 being essential for taking the war to mainland Japan and that in turn served the broader objectives of both air and naval forces. The B-36 would be handy to have against the day that the B-29 failed to fulfil its objective, or the war went on into the latter half of the 1940s. It was also a tool which could serve as a deterrent against

aggression from a belligerent power after the war with Nazi Germany had been won and Imperial Japan defeated.

There was already awareness of threats to the United States from the Soviet Union, the relationship between the two countries before Russia was attacked by Germany in June 1941 being lukewarm at best. The anti-capitalist, Bolshevik state being in ideological conflict with the freedom-loving Americans and their consumer-based society, controlled at opposite ends of the spectrum by financiers on Wall St and politicians in Congress, only consensually managed by the President in the White House. As war-fever gripped industry and took control of the national economy, there was disquiet among particular circles that Stalin was leading Russia to ultimate victory and a future world in which there would be another contest and one in which the United States might have to fight again, across oceans separating adversaries.

In 1943, AAF leaders debated the challenge faced by such a post-war scenario for which the B-36 could be a winning tool as both deterrent and intercontinental bomb-truck. Political debate surrounded the value of the B-36 which was considered a priority for post-war adaptation of military requirements in a peacetime economy. The urgent need to make an irreversible commitment to the B-36 was verified

MORS AB ALTO

NO SMOKING WITHIN 100 FT

by the assistant chief of the air staff, Major General Echols when he said that: "the ordinary procedure would result in a delay of one year in production... and it was very possible that the war would be over before production could commence."

Supporters in Congress pointed to the economics of this giant aircraft which, despite its high procurement price, worked well in its favour, promising half the operating cost per ton/mile of the B-29. There was never a better opportunity to employ the overall war economy on fast-track development of the B-36. When Japan attacked Pearl Harbor US defence spending was 2.4% of GDP, rising to 32% in 1943 and 45% the following year. But the 'industrial military complex' of which President Roosevelt was so proud could afford it and the manufacturing and production capacity of the American war machine was amply equipped to develop and deploy the type.

Testimony before the political leadership during these crucial years for the B-36 reminded the decision-makers that only through an abundance of overwhelming force could the United States rest easy and deter a future attack by another power. It was necessary to fund the tools for that future in the industrial capabilities of a nation already on a war-footing and with funds available greater than perhaps at any other time in the future. Moreover, the senior military leadership was aware of the Manhattan Project developing the first atomic bomb and for that the long range and superior weight-lifting capability of the B-36 would expand the global reach.

Shortly after the production contract had been awarded in July 1943 delays began to build and the anticipated first flight of May 1944 was clearly slipping. And, by the beginning of that year the date had moved to June 1945. In

those two years there were significant changes to the aerofoil design and a wing flutter issue brought further concerns and redesign work. With the imminent availability of atomic weapons, the AAF was determined to push through these problems and bring the type to operational readiness as soon as possible. However, with advancing technology and the emerging generation of radio and radar equipment, trialled in many cases by the B-29, the concurrency approach proved troublesome for their integration with the B-36 while detailed design was still in progress for an aircraft expected to enter full-scale production shortly after the flight test phase. This too slowed development through to completion of the first airframes and additional radar equipment alone added 3,500lb (1,588kg) to the empty weight.

Counter to the effort made by aerodynamicists to achieve a clean airframe free of drag, were the bulges and fairings necessary to fit electronic

systems and design engineers worked to place the Western Electric AN/APQ-7 Eagle radar antenna into the leading edge of the wing to maintain a smooth exterior. Eagle radar equipment had been fitted to some B-24 and B-29 aircraft which carried an antenna mounted transversely under the fuselage giving the appearance of an additional wing. This would have seriously compromised the performance of the B-36, but its incorporation proved unnecessary as it was replaced by the APQ-23, X-band, high-altitude bombing radar, a type also fitted to some B-29s, including *Enola Gay* which dropped the atomic bomb on Hiroshima.

Weight was becoming a serious problem as the programme fought against delays, many of which were caused by the AAF changing its mind on certain items of equipment and introducing the latest, or the most available, systems and

TOP: *Fitted to the XB-36 (49-13570), the 110in (279.4cm) tyre was impractical due to wing stowage requirements and the damaging runway overpressure.* Via Dennis Jenkins

ABOVE: *The single-wheel main landing gear under test, a concept quickly abandoned in favour of a multi-wheel bogie arrangement.* Via Dennis Jenkins

LEFT: *The redesigned main landing gear incorporated a four-wheel bogie for lower overpressure and better wing stowage, a design subsequently adopted for other aircraft.* Via Dennis Jenkins

1. OLEO STRUT
2. FILLER PLUG
3. EQUALIZER ASSEMBLY
4. FAIRING
5. POSITIONING JACK
6. AIR VALVE
7. MAIN COLUMN
8. OUTBOARD TRUSS TUBE
9. INBOARD TRUSS TUBE
10. PIVOT SHAFT
11. MAIN DRAG STRUT
12. AUXILIARY DRAG STRUT
13. MAIN ACTUATING CYLINDER
14. AUXILIARY ACTUATING CYLINDER
15. LATCH LINK ROD
16. INDICATOR FLAG
17. LATCH LINK PIN
18. LATCH
19. SIDE BRACE
20. HYDRAULIC SNUBBER
21. FIXED LINK

*ABOVE: **Struts and truss assemblies for the revised bogie leg on the B-36 folded the gear into a smaller recess than that required for the single-wheel configuration.** Convair*

*RIGHT: **Never likely to be successful, tests were carried out with a tracked landing gear for better load distribution on contact with the runway, clearly unsuitable as parts of the track were shed all along the runway.** Convair*

subsystems. Trouble with the engines at this time also made weight-saving measures problematic, modifications to the X-Wasp adding a further 2,304lb (1,045kg) overall.

Potentially more serious was the main landing gear for the tricycle undercarriage. As originally designed, the aircraft would have one tyre each side with a diameter of 110in (279cm), at 1,475lb (669kg) the largest tyres manufactured by the contractor, Goodyear. Each had a 225lb (102kg) inner tube pressurised to 100psi (689.5kPa). The wheels were 46in (116.8cm) in diameter, weighing 850lb (385kg) to which were attached triple-disc brake units each weighing 735lb (333.3kg) for a total wheel assembly that added 8,550lb (3,878kg) to the overall weight of the aircraft, considerably more than the weight of a P-51D Mustang.

Optimised in design to fit the undercarriage into the wing space, the single wheel each side imposed too great a weight on the runway, only three

in the world being capable of supporting the enormous weight of the aircraft, which required a concrete depth of at least 22in (55.9cm). All three runways (Fort Worth, Texas, Eglin Field, Florida, and Fairfield-Suisun Field, California) were in the continental United States and there were already plans to deploy the B-36 overseas for which there were no suitable runways. A bigger risk was the consequences of a blown tyre on landing, potentially catastrophic for the aircraft.

A solution was sought by Major General Edward M Powers, the Assistant Chief of Air Staff for Materiel, Maintenance and Distribution who worked with Consolidated to design a multi-wheel bogie of a unique type which would serve as the genesis for a new and evolving design of landing gear and become a standard concept for many aircraft types several decades later. The B-36 design adopted a four-wheel unit each side with 56in (142.4cm) tyres in a compact arrangement which, nevertheless, being bulkier in side elevation, necessitated a bulge in the upper wing and in the wheel well doors to accommodate it. Yet these drag-inducing bulges were offset to some extent by the 2,600lb

(1,179kg) saving in weight over the original design.

While at its inception the B-36 had been considered as a Euro-bomber, the war with Japan had accelerated production of the B-29 and projected roles now envisaged it as a post-war strategic bomber and deterrent. With that consideration, a small unit from the AAF conducted a study of potential landing strips which could be used for staging back to the United States after a deep-strike into enemy territory and for that clearly Russia was the target. There was no consideration of aerial refuelling, which would come immediately after the war with Japan was over, and there was no means by which the B-36 could be adapted to receive an in-flight top-up.

As noted in a later chapter (Planning Armageddon), bases in England, the Middle East and occupied Japan were key places from where to stage the B-36 and support requirements were assessed accordingly. The runway footprint load had been satisfied with the change in the configuration of the landing gear but there would be significant requirements placed on foreign bases to keep the B-36 flying. These analyses favoured the use of US military transport aircraft to carry support equipment, spare parts, including engines and the essential personnel to maintain and service the aircraft. Which, with its gargantuan size, required special ladders, gantries and lifting devices to fuel and bomb-up the B-36 wherever it was deployed.

By the end of the war, these teams had a clear idea of what was required from the bomber groups equipped with the B-36 and from the transport wings committed to support for the overall deployment. Although capable of intercontinental range, access to facilities abroad would be essential and this aircraft paved the way for later deployments of B-47 and B-52 types, each of which were developed for dispersal to foreign locations and integration with local facilities and personnel. An unsung contribution to the ultimate deployment of strategic air power assets around the globe.

The Challengers

Two flying wing contenders from Northrop competed for the contract to build America's next strategic bomber.

Northrop XB-35

On May 27, 1941, the AAF awarded a contract to Northrop for two XB-35 prototypes and 13 YB-35 flying-wing aircraft with a production contract for 200 in December 1942. With a promise of eliminating excess drag, the concept was novel but lacking in wind tunnel tests. Nothing presented by Northrop could have satisfactorily assured the AAF of its success. Yet the B-35 programme is significant to the story of the B-36 in that it was its greatest challenger. It was also unique as a bomber concept.

Formed in August 1939 by John K 'Jack' Northrop at the end of a 10-year period developing flying-wing concepts, the company lacked the resources for serial production, so the AAF integrated the Glenn L Martin Company to support the contract. Northrop wanted to learn more about the flying-wing concept, and it built four 30% scale N-9M types to evaluate the flying qualities and handling characteristics of the full size XB-35.

The first crashed in May 1943 and most of the 45 flights it made were terminated due to mechanical failures. The second N-9M took to the air in June 1943 and the first drag data on the flying wing was obtained that September. But this was bad news when tests showed a 9-12% increase in drag compared to wind tunnel tests. Also, serious stability and directional control problems were encountered, with spin control, stall characteristics and control at low speeds all indicating major issues.

With production having begun a year before test data from the N-9M revealed serious flaws, the XB-35 became the ultimate example of the folly of concurrency. Originally scheduled for late 1943, the first flight was delayed by more than three years and in May 1945 the AAF cancelled the contract and allowed work to proceed only on the two XB-35 prototypes and the 13 YB-35s ordered in May 1941. Along with poor aero-performance, escalating costs added to the aircraft's nemesis. In 1941 the prototyping phase was estimated to cost $4.45m; three years later the total programme had grown to an estimated $25m.

Beset by problems pointedly down to concurrency and the compressed, overlapping cycle of design, assembly, and modification, the first XB-35 would not fly before June 25, 1946.

Despite its failings, the XB-35 introduced several unique features driven by its sheer size, although it had a relatively conventional swept-back cantilever wing of aluminium-alloy constructed in a single piece and straight tapered. But it had eight separate bomb bays and a crew of 15, six beds and a fully pressurised crew compartment.

Significant changes had been introduced during the second half of 1948 with the contract modified to include five YB-35s and four YB-35As each powered by Allison J35-A-17 jet engines. One YB-35A was assigned to static tests, a second was to be the prototype for

an RB-35 reconnaissance version, and a third was to have been the testbed for a Turbodyne T-7 turboprop engine. The second XB-35 was earmarked for a flexible mounted gear box to damp oscillations from the single-rotation propellers, but costs prevented these from being implemented.

The programme was cancelled in August 1949 and two months later the air staff dropped plans to convert YB-35 and YB-35A aircraft, despite the two XB-35s and the 13 YB-35s having been paid for. The rest of the production lot had been scrapped by March 1950

ABOVE: Jack Northrop spent a life advocating the flying wing concept for low-drag, aerodynamically efficient aircraft and developed the XB-35 as a candidate for the long-range bomber requirement which took to the air for the first time in June 1946. Northrop

BELOW: Compromised by inadequate flight control and stabilisation electronics, the XB-35 failed expectations due to instability and a lower performance than predicted. Northrop

more than 20 months, the two aircraft completed 169 flights, demonstrating a maximum speed of 520mph (837kph) with a service ceiling of 42,000ft (12,800m). The aircraft had a range of 4,000 miles (6,400km) carrying a 10,000lb (4,536kg) bomb load, half the range of the XB-35.

But the stability problems were still there and never completely corrected, the aircraft being useless as a stable bombing platform due to violent pitching and yawing. In March 1948 Northrop proposed a reconnaissance version, the YRB-49A and the US Air Force accepted this with an order for 30 aircraft on August 12. Ironically, on June 5 the second YB-49 had crashed north of Muroc killing the pilot Captain Edwards and four other crewmembers. Muroc was renamed Edwards Air Force Base in his honour. The YRB-49A would have had six Allison J35-A19 jet engines in the wings, two on each side, and two more suspended in pods beneath the wing leading edge.

Lacking confidence in Northrop to handle such a major production contract, in December 1948 the US Air Force cancelled the entire programme. The sole YRB-49A built flew for the first time on May 4, 1950, and continued to fly until early 1952 when it was flown to Northrop's Ontario International Airport for installation of a stability augmentation system. By this time funds had run out and it remained there until scrapped in November 1953.

ABOVE: Seen here on its first flight in October 1947, the YB-49 gave jet power to the tailless flying wing but remained unsuited to the demanding role for which it was designed. Northrop

and the type disappeared into history, followed too by the unsuccessful YB-49 which was intended to be the jet-powered successor.

Northrop YB-49

The second and third YB-35s were converted under a contract signed on June 1, 1945. The original four Wasp engines were replaced by eight Allison J35-A-5 turbojets each rated at 4,000lb (18kN) and buried in the wing, four either side of the centre-section to the forward end of which was the cockpit. Low drag intakes were designed into the wing leading edge.

The control and handling difficulties were alleviated with the provision of four vertical stub-tails extending just above and below the wing inboard and outboard of the engine groups. Wing fences were added for additional stability, extending forward from the vertical fins to the leading edge to apply the stabilising effect previously provided by the propellers and shaft housings. A crew of seven was contained within the centre-section of the wing with the pilot located centrally beneath a bubble canopy.

The first of the two converted aircraft made its initial flight on October 21, 1947, more than a year after the planned date due to engineering problems with the design of the vertical fins. It was joined for its test programme at Muroc AFB by the second aircraft on January 13, 1948. Over a period of

Equipped with six Allison jet engines, the YRB-49A flew in May 1950, by this date employed only for flight tests with the flying wing design. Northrop

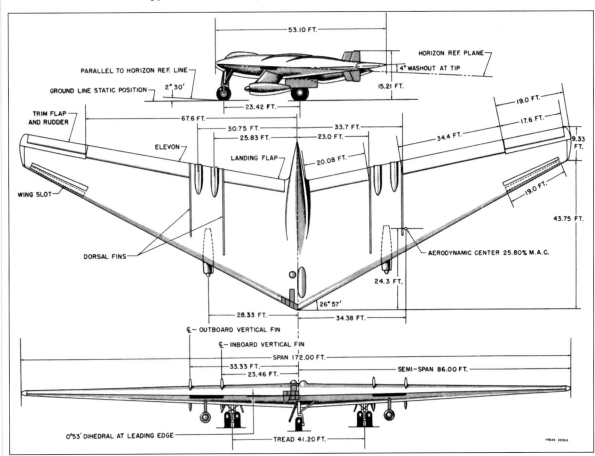

Strategic Air Command

The B-36 would be the mainstay of America's global atomic reach for its first decade, but the origin of that force was far from inevitable.

USAAF Bomber Command began operations against the Japanese mainland in August 1944, the B-29 playing a truly decisive role in the inevitable outcome of World War Two. Before the two atomic raids on Hiroshima and Nagasaki, 91% of all bombs dropped on Japan had been carried to their targets by this aircraft, burning out 66% of all urban areas and virtually halting any meaningful continuation of the war. It is no overstatement to say that the performance of this aircraft in that war

FAR LEFT: *With the proud motto 'Peace is our Profession', the badge of Strategic Air Command depicted the mailed fist clutching a lightning bolt. USAF*

LEFT: *Curtis LeMay served as Commander in Chief SAC (CINCSAC) from 1948 to 1957, honing America's strategic air arm into a highly respected fighting force with the B-36 bearing the burden of retribution throughout his tenure in post. USAF*

RIGHT: *The 1,000th B-29 completed at the Wichita, Kansas, production line rolls out to a greeting by company employees.* Boeing

BELOW: *Before the B-36 entered service in 1948, the B-29 held a lead role in maintaining a strong deterrent, its design and production record serving as a stimulus to post-war planning for a strategic bomber force.* Boeing

did much to instil in the armed services and the public at large that strategic air power would be crucial to success in future wars and that, for the time being at least, the B-29 would be a critical national asset and a precursor to the B-36.

In March 1946 the reorganisation of the USAAF retired the Continental Air Forces (CAF), which had only been in existence since December 15, 1944, to relieve the air staff of operational duties in the United States and allow more time for policy decisions. The first units for the CAF were assigned on April 16, 1945, and it commanded operational control of them from May 10, 1945. In March 1946 three new commands were set up, of which one was Strategic Air Command (SAC), the other two being Air Defense Command (ADC) and Tactical Air Command (TAC).

SAC officially came into existence on March 12, 1946 with a clear mandate to deliver a strategic response to unprovoked aggression and to integrate the deployment of both conventional and atomic weapons. Headquarters Second AF was deactivated on March 30, 1946, and Headquarters Fifteenth AF was assigned to SAC, effective the following day from Colorado Springs, Colorado, absorbing all its personnel and equipment. At the end of March 1946, SAC had 55 airfields and installations and 43 of those went to the Fifteenth AF, but most of these had been left over from wartime use.

As the only operational command in SAC, the Fifteenth had the strategic B-29s but they were in varying states of readiness with no ability to operate effectively in a combat situation for several weeks. General George C Kenney was given command of SAC, a position which he served in from March 21, 1946, to October 19, 1948. Brigadier General Charles F Born was in command of Fifteenth AF until April 15, 1947.

Three important units were VIII Bomber Command (VH) at Peterson Field, Colorado Springs, the 58th Very Heavy Bombardment Wing assigned atomic bomb duties, and the 73rd Very Heavy Bombardment Wing at MacDill Army Air Field, Florida. Below wing level came the 509th Composite Group of the 58th Very Heavy Bombardment Wing at Roswell Army Air Base, New Mexico, and the 12 Very Heavy Bombardment Groups assigned to SAC from the outset.

The 311th Reconnaissance Wing was assigned to Fifteenth AF from August 1 and the Eighth AF, operating under Headquarters Fifteenth AF, moved from MacDill to Fort Worth Army Air Field on November 1. VIII Bomber Command had been tasked with Operation Wonderful, the administrative management of six Very Heavy Bomber and tactical and service units of the Second AF assigned to overseas duty. This came to an end on November 10 due to administrative objections from overseas commanders.

Operational Challenges

On August 9, 1946, an American C-47 was shot down over Yugoslavia, followed by another incident several hours later from ground fire bringing vigorous protest from the US Department of State. RAF Spitfires were sent up from the Klagenfurt area to try to find the second aircraft but without success. A flight of six B-29s from the 43rd BG at Davis-Monthan Field, Arizona led by Colonel James C Selser Jr, flew to Rhein-Main Airfield, Germany, in mid-November 1946.

Accompanied by two C-54s of the 1st Air Transport Unit out of Roswell Field, New Mexico, and with B-29s carrying spares and equipment, they remained there for two weeks and conducted several flights along Russian-occupied territory. They also visited airfields in Western Europe to judge their suitability for supporting the B-29 in the event of deployment there in what is regarded as the first use of this aircraft as an instrument of international diplomacy.

Several months later, while SAC did not contribute directly to the Berlin airlift after the Russians imposed a blockade, it played a vital role in projecting US willingness to stand up to Soviet aggression and because it was the single instrument of strategic air capability, the B-29 played an important part. The 28th and 307th VHBGs were placed on alert readiness for moving across the Atlantic Ocean. The 301st had all three of its squadrons in Germany by the beginning of July while the 28th BG moved from Rapid City AFB, South Dakota, to RAF Scampton, England, and the 307th went from MacDill AFB, Florida, to RAF Marham and RAF Waddington.

LEFT: *General Thomas 'Tommy' Power (foreground) and General Bernard Schriever during a US Senate hearing. Power succeeded LeMay as CINCSAC from 1957 to 1964. USAF*

All deployments had been completed by July 17 and the alert status for the other groups was stood down. The deployments caused the squadrons to remain on standby, which prevented them from conducting training and familiarisation flights and that interfered with general operational exercises. The 301st was replaced by the 2nd BG which went to England, but it returned to mainland Europe to replace the 28th BG. Deployments to England under Project Looker were the first since World War Two and had been delayed somewhat by the need for procedures to be agreed with national and local authorities.

Also, because of essential arrangements in facilities and supporting equipment, airfields that had not been expected to support American bombers were hastily made available. Deployed to the UK under Operation Dagger, the 307th BG had previously been conducting antisubmarine training but with one squadron at Waddington and two at Scampton the opportunity was taken to carry out interception by RAF fighters against B-29s conducting a simulated attack on London during Battle of Britain Week, 13-19 September.

The group returned to MacDill AFB on November 2, replaced by the 22nd BG. For the British, the period of the Berlin airlift had special poignancy. In contributing to the supply of grain, ships bound for Britain were redirected to German ports at the government's request and rationing was re-introduced, the first time that staple

BELOW: *The B-36 never went to war in anger, but the Korean War (1950-1953) provided lessons for developing SAC and its long-range bomber, a B-29 from the 307th BG here in action dropping bombs on North Korea. SAC*

ABOVE: *Converted into a tanker role, the KB-29J was the last strategic bomber to be so adapted, the B-36 having no role to play in this requirement which would expand greatly when mid-air refuelling extended the range of its successors.* USAF

foods had been rationed in the UK, even in wartime. At US-occupied British bases, airmen again hosted parties for local children, as they had frequently done during the war.

The emergency deployments of 1948 were sustained until the Russians backed down and supply routes to Berlin from Western Europe opened once more. The reduction was gradual, ensuring that at least one full group remained in England from August 1949. But the requirement for a rapid mobilisation had a profound effect on planning for future, unforeseen eventualities and that became more important after the Russians detonated their first atomic bomb on August 29, 1949.

In 1948 SAC had 837 aircraft on strength of which 486 were B-29s and 30 were RB-29 reconnaissance types, 35 were B-50s and 35 were B-36s. It was a memorable year in which the capability of SAC increased considerably with the imminent arrival of the first Boeing B-50A on February 20 and the Convair B-36A on June 26. These aircraft signalled a step change

in both operations and war-planning potential, although the lack of atomic weapons still emphasised SAC's conventional bombing role.

The B-29 had been categorised as a 'very heavy bomber' (VHB) but with the arrival of the much improved B-50 and the massive B-36, this category was dropped and both B-29 and B-50 types were re-categorised as medium bombers while the B-36 was to be a heavy bomber type, But there were disquieting reports of a command in crisis. Much of the equipment carried by the B-29 was inherited from World War Two and the performance of radar equipment was threatened by outdated components, many fearing that they could be easily jammed.

Responding to these deep concerns about the inadequate state of readiness displayed by SAC over the Berlin crisis, and to both political and Pentagon concerns about his leadership, on October 19, 1948, Kenney was replaced by Curtis LeMay and a week later Thomas D Power replaced McMullen, who was reassigned as commanding general of the San Antonio Air Material

area. Kenney was transferred to command of the Air University at Maxwell Field. LeMay would remain in command of SAC until June 30, 1957, when he was replaced by 'Tommy' Power, who held command until November 30, 1964. Together, LeMay and Power would hone SAC into one of the most respected and envied combat commands in the history of US air power, the one most feared by the Soviet Union.

Immediately after receiving command of SAC, LeMay went to Andrews AFB outside Washington DC, where he discovered that there was not one crew that could: "do a professional job. Not one of the outfits was up to strength – neither in airplanes nor in people nor anything else." LeMay's goal was clear, in that SAC "had to be ready to go to war not next week, not tomorrow, but this afternoon, today…We had to operate every day as if we were at war," adding that he would not settle for anything less than a force "so professional, so strong, so powerful, that we would not have to fight."

Despite 1948 being a challenging year, several notable flights took place in an attempt to demonstrate the range and long-duration capability of SAC's aircraft. On July 29 the 43rd BG sent three B-29s from Davis-Monthan on an attempted flight around the world. Planned to take 14 days, it was extended by a day when one aircraft crashed into the Arabian Sea. The circumnavigation was completed in 103hrs 50min flying time by the two remaining aircraft, one commanded by Lieutenant Colonel R W Kline and the other by 1st Lieutenant A M Neal, landing back at base on August 6.

RIGHT: *A KB-29J refuels a FJ-4B from VMA-214 as a further application when its primary role as a bomber was supplanted by the B-50 and the B-36.* USAF

Bombing accuracy was key to a successful mission in real-world situations and LeMay was concerned at the poor record demonstrated to date. In January 1949 a simulated radar bombing mission was conducted against Dayton, Ohio, in which only 71 out of 101 B-29s assigned actually left the ground. Only 303 bombing runs were completed at an altitude of 30,000ft (9,100m) rather than the usual 10,000-15,000ft (3,048-4,572m), two-thirds getting no closer to their targets than 10,090ft (3,075m). Aiming had been seriously compromised by the freezing conditions, heavy rain, and thick cloud. Frustrated, LeMay remarked that not one aircraft had completed its planned mission. Had this been the miss distance over Hiroshima or Nagasaki, the target cities would have been left unscathed.

The blast wave and fireball of a Mk III implosion-type atom bomb was insufficient to achieve desired results should the detonation distance be greater than 2,000ft (610m) from the target. While much had been made by the public and the press in general about the destructive potential of fission bombs, in reality they were not as destructive as had been assumed and the ability of a SAC bomber to get within 1,000ft (305m) was essential, given the type of material against which the bomb would be detonated.

When To Go To War?

The threat posed by the Soviet bomb ran deep, challenging the confidence in military superiority which the Truman administration had believed it had bestowed upon the American public. The shock news about inefficiencies made headlines and politicians wanted answers. There were delicate issues in the reaction to this news and in a highly

Bombers in the SAC inventory during the period 1947-1959 covering B-36 in service.						
Year	B-29/RB-29	B-50/RB-50	B-36/RB-36	B-45	B-47/RB-47	B-52
1947	319	0	0	0	0	0
1948	516	35	35	0	0	0
1949	452	99	36	0	0	0
1950	431	215	58	27	0	0
1951	370	259	163	38	12	0
1952	435	263	268	22	62	0
1953	118	176	322	0	329	0
1954	0	90	342	0	1,060	0
1955	0	12	338	0	1,320	18
1956	0	0	247	0	1,560	97
1957	0	0	127	0	1,501	243
1958	0	0	22	0	1,543	380
1959	0	0	0	0	1,540	488

Note: The above exclude tankers, transport or fighter types.

classified letter to Vandenberg, on December 12, 1949, LeMay debated the value of a pre-emptive or preventative war, a first strike on the Soviet Union to destroy its war-fighting capability before it could be deployed. Citing a need to follow what he perceived to be Vandenberg's position, LeMay stressed: "the importance of accelerating our readiness to conduct effective atomic warfare."

LeMay also worried about what he perceived to be the threat of a Soviet first-strike, given "the information available to us," adding the chilling thought that "it is unlikely that we can prevent the Soviets from attaining a measure of success in any attacks against our striking force...we have little or no margin of safety." Moreover, he asserted, "it would appear economical and logical to adopt the objective of completely avoiding enemy attack against our strategic force by destroying his atomic force before it can attack ours."

It has never been declassified, but the views expressed by Vandenberg and the degree to which LeMay acquiesced, or indeed initiated the discussion regarding a pre-emptive strike to neutralise Soviet war-making capabilities is not currently known. Under LeMay, the entire structure of SAC would be orientated toward a deterrent. His disclosed response to Vandenberg is illuminating, in that it presupposes the validity of the premise while shaping it to the laws of war and the belief in political circles that the United States should not initiate a conflict through first-strike or pre-emptive means:

"Assuming that as a democracy we are not prepared to wage a preventive war, this course of action poses two most difficult requirements: (1) An intelligence system which can locate the vulnerable elements of the Soviet striking force and forewarn us when attack by that force is imminent, and (2) Agreement at

LEFT: *In parallel with the early post-war period, SAC operated a few North American B-45s, the first US jet bomber to enter service.* USAF

RIGHT: *With a B-36 in the background, the YB-52 visits Carswell AFB, having made its first flight in 1952. It would be operational with SAC in 1955. USAF*

top governmental level that when such information is received the Strategic Air Command will be directed to attack."

Within these exchanges and the letter of December 12, 1949, is the reason why LeMay placed considerable emphasis on the reconnaissance role and why he pushed hard for such a mission attached to the incoming B-36 and the B-47. All the while maintaining a strong role for both photographic and signals intelligence-gathering missions on the border with, and at times inside, the Soviet Union and its occupied territories. In that he would find common ground with Dwight D Eisenhower when serving as President from January 1952 to January 1961, the most 'intelligence-orientated' occupant of the White House in history.

In 1949 intensive training of B-29 and B-50 crews began and, as part of the improvements to crew operations in bombing tests and simulated attacks, a Lead Crew School was set up at Walker AFB, New Mexico. This was already showing improvements over the previous year. In addition, to give crews the experience of living and working overseas, selected bases hosted personnel on rotation from the United States. The stress of these activities intentionally placed crews in a pseudo-combat environment and the persistent problem with housing and general facilities at numerous places around the world posed problems. However, 50% of those discharged at the end of their term of service returned to fill their vacated slots. This was more than many commanders expected but far less than had been hoped for.

BELOW: *The all-jet B-47 medium bomber which joined SAC in 1952, ushering in a new era six years before the B-36 retired, its successor being the eight-engine B-52. USAF*

Keen to stretch the global wings of its new and potent B-50A, an aircraft from the 43rd BG (46-010 *Lucky Lady II*) completed a flight around the world on March 2, logging 23,452 miles

(37,734km) in 94hr 1min carrying a crew of 14 commanded by Captain J Gallagher from Carswell AFB. The aircraft had been refuelled in the air four times by KB-29 tankers of the 43rd Air Refuelling Squadron. The achievement attracted numerous awards for the crew and the event itself won the Mackay Trophy for 1949, presented each year by the National Aeronautic Association for a feat of outstanding national accomplishment.

Just 10 days after the B-50 returned, a B-36 of the 7th BG arrived back at its home base of Fort Worth, Texas, having flown 9,600 miles (15,446km) in 43hr 7min without refuelling. It had been flown by a crew of 12 commanded by Captain Roy Showalter. This flight was one of many being conducted to evaluate the performance of this new behemoth, providing vital information on speed, high-altitude performance and weight carrying capacity as well as to assess the effectiveness of the comprehensive air armament and to conduct simulated penetration of enemy defences.

On April 6, 1949, the 3rd Air Division came under SAC for its rotational duties to the UK and its commanding general,

Major General Leon W Johnson, reported directly to headquarters USAF and to LeMay. On November 1, the Second AF was activated at Barksdale AFB, Louisiana, and assigned to SAC Headquarters with personnel from the 311th Air Division relocated from Forbes AFB, Kansas, when that unit was disbanded. Six days later, the Fifteenth AF headquarters moved from Ent AFB, Colorado, to March AFB, California.

That year saw a major transition in aircraft types, paper returns showing 868 tactical aircraft of which there were 390 B-29s, 62 RB-29s, 67 KB-29s, 99 B-50s and 36 B-36s. Three heavy bomb groups were equipped with the B-36 and 11 medium bomber groups operated the B-29 and the B-50, while two fighter groups had the F-86 and the F-82. Three reconnaissance groups had RB-29s, 18 RB-17s and C-82s and two strategic support squadrons had C-54s and YC-97s while six air refuelling squadrons operated the KB-29s in their new role. In all, during 1949 SAC had 17 bases in the United States. Overall, SAC had 71,490 officers, airmen and civilians, up more than one-third on 1948.

Planning Armageddon

With the aircraft to deliver them being constantly refined, Strategic Air Command began the cold duty of planning how and where to deploy their atomic arsenal.

The US strategic bombing campaign of World War Two was a template for the core function of the post-war, independent US Air Force of which the B-36 would be at the heart of any military response to Soviet aggression. Planning began on August 4, 1945, two days before the atomic bomb was dropped on Hiroshima, when the Joint Strategic Survey Committee (JSSC) and the Joint War Plans Committee (JWPC) requested a strategic plan for US military roles and responsibilities after the war.

They consulted with Major General Leslie Groves, director of the Manhattan atomic bomb programme, and Dr Vannevar Bush, chairman of the Joint Committee on New Weapons and Equipment. Dr Bush had been running the Office of Scientific Research and Development (OSRD) since 1941 and had administered Manhattan. He met with the group on August 22 to give his opinion on what weapons might be available and how that might influence planning. It was important in the planning stage to define the type and capabilities of weapons concerned so as to estimate the location of operating and support bases.

The first attempt to provide a war plan began when the JWPC distributed a discussion paper on April 13 providing several different studies indicating the number of occupation forces required for Europe and the Middle East and for deployment to the Far East together with a list of air bases required. Named 'Pincher', the study did not identify the initial use of atomic weapons due to their scarcity, but it acknowledged that they could be critical in any future war. It was the basis for a Joint Basic War Plan which interleaved with similar plans from the US Army and the US Navy and was approved for basic planning on June 18.

Further work under Pincher produced several separate plans for different global sectors and on July 16, 1947, the JWPC informed the JPS that it was ready to prepare a combined war-fighting plan for conflict with the Soviet Union. These plans were adjusted over time to input the changing capabilities of SAC aircraft, bombs, and flight planning, factors which controlled what could be done in an atomic war and in a strategic conflict also involving conventional weapons.

Between 1945 and 1949 the medium, heavy, and very-heavy bomber categories would change due to the introduction of the B-50 and the B-36 in 1948 and the imminent availability of the all-jet B-47. During the Pincher studies, the assistant chief of the air staff for plans began to develop a strategic plan it could pull out to instantly mobilise at the onset of conflict all the various elements, commands, units, bases, equipment, munitions, and personnel required. It allowed flexible options down interconnecting chains of command.

Named 'Makefast', the plan was based on tried and tested plans from World War Two and focused on a strategic bombing campaign against petroleum resources and on refining and distribution of fuel, without specific reference to targeted population centres or major cities. The fluid nature of Makefast required continual updating and a new version, completed in February 1947, and named 'Earshot', further modified to 'Earshot Junior' that summer, was named Operation Plan OPLAN 14-47.

By this time, the JWPC had decided that sufficient work had already been done to justify a concentrated plan for attacks on the Soviet Union within the next three years and this was authorised on August 29, 1947, by the Joint Strategic Plans Committee (JSPC)

ABOVE: *A photo-shoot to demonstrate SAC's migration from the B-36 (right) to the B-52 (bottom) and the supersonic B-58, all three the ultimate deterrent. USAF*

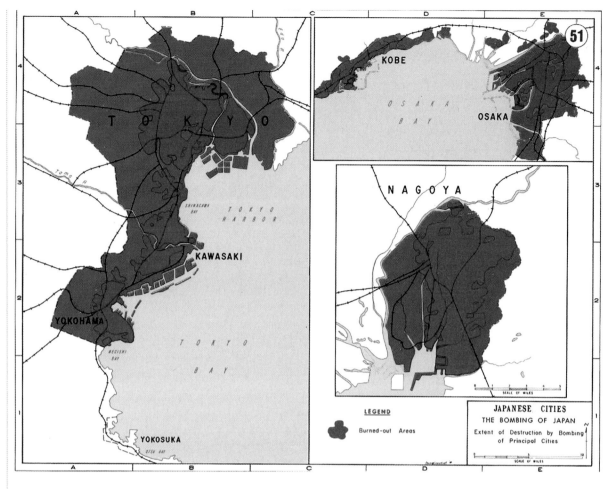

RIGHT: *Assessment of the damage incurred by strategic bombing on Japanese cities during World War Two included the Tokyo firestorm raids.* USAF

LEGEND
Burned-out Areas

JAPANESE CITIES
THE BOMBING OF JAPAN
Extent of Destruction by Bombing of Principal Cities

SCALE OF MILES

BELOW: *The Castle Bravo nuclear test of March 1, 1954, provided vital information as the first high-yield detonation, exceeding the predicted 6MT to release 15MT of energy with disastrous consequences for the inhabitants near Bikini Atoll in the Pacific Ocean.* USAF

which on enactment of the National Security Act had replaced the Joint Staff Planners. It carried the codename 'Broiler' and assumed the use of atomic weapons from the outset.

Unlike Pincher, it embraced the destruction of civil infrastructure; atomic weapons would have to be used in an attack on the cities. Through Broiler the outflow of collateral advantage from using atomic weapons began to take hold. It dawned on planners that if a whole city became a legitimate target, the population of workers themselves became a military target and the Air Force Intelligence Directorate posed the question: "What was a city besides a collection of industry?"

Presented on November 8, 1947, Broiler was disturbingly ahead of the resources it would need to draw upon. The sheer scale of the undertaking was far beyond the men and the machines available when it envisaged use of atomic weapons from the outset in a war theorised to begin in 1948. It would start, said the theorists, with bombing strikes delivered from bases in the United States, the UK, and the Middle East, with 34 atomic bombs dropped on 24 cities. Seven would be dropped on Moscow, three on Leningrad, two on Kharkov and Stalingrad and single bombs on other cities. Overall, it assumed availability of 100-200 atomic bombs when not even half that number would be available by mid-1948.

When Broiler planners drafted their strategies, only the B-29 and the B-50 were available. The B-36 was not yet entering SAC and by the end of 1947 it had only 32 aircraft capable of carrying the atomic bomb with 20% of Soviet targets beyond the range of even the closest air bases. The solution was to fly one-way missions which was justified by Major General Earl Partridge when he proposed to "Expend the crew, expend the bomb, expend the airplane all at once. Kiss them goodbye and let them go," and when reflecting on that decision, admitting that it was "a pretty cold blooded point of view," conceding that he "believed that it is economically best for the country."

If a war broke out, 1949 being the earliest date now envisaged, B-36s would fly bombing missions from the United States while B-29s and the B-50s would fly out of the UK, Cairo, and Okinawa. The National Security Council adopted a resolution on September 16, specifically approving the use of atomic weapons at any time should war break out. Targeting would give priority to petroleum production, the top 10 refineries in Russia being hit and taken out of action in the first 70 objectives during which 72% of total Soviet capacity would be eliminated. SAC would use conventional attacks to destroy transportation networks, hydro-electric plants, ports, and waterways, with coastal areas mined to prevent maritime movement and inhibit naval operations.

The Armed Forces Special Weapons Project (AFSWP) was responsible for assembling and delivering atomic bombs to where they were needed. Special expeditionary buildings existed for transport to overseas bases. When erected, the expeditionary building for installing atomic bombs measured 20ft (6.1m) by 100ft (30.5m) in size and the extensive attention to war plans encouraged special procedures for conveying, assembling, and fitting these weapons. However, a major problem responsible for slowing down readiness levels at SAC was the convoluted way in which bombs would be delivered to the aircraft.

Accessing Bombs

Atom bombs were stored at Sandia Base, operated by the Sandia Corporation of Albuquerque, New Mexico, and the only loading site in the United States was at Kirtland AFB, New Mexico. Construction of six National Stockpile Sites (NSSs) began in 1947, with Site A adjacent to Kirtland and Sandia, Site B alongside Gray AFB, Texas, and Site C at Clarksville

Base, Fort Campbell, on the Kentucky/ Tennessee border. Other NSSs were located at: Bossier Base, Barksdale, Louisiana; Lake Mead Base at Nellis AFB, Nevada; and Medina Base at Lakeland AFB, Texas.

All were operational by the end of 1949 when the B-36 was entering service, supplemented by seven Operational Storage Sites (OSSs). NSS and OSS facilities were controlled by the Atomic Energy Commission (AEC) and the Armed Forces Special Weapons Project (AFSWP). The AFSWP worked closely with Sandia Laboratories' Z-Division to develop procedures for the supply of bombs. To handle the bombs, Special Weapons Units (SWEs) were set up each with 77 individuals on constant alert through rotation ready to deploy anywhere in the world to assemble and install a bomb for flight in a B-29, a B-50, or a B-36.

Under development at this date, the Mk IV was designed for ease of assembly and a dialled yield from 1KT to 31KT, approximately 0.7-210% of the yield of the uranium-235 'gun' type bomb dropped on Hiroshima. Almost the same explosive package as in the Mk III, the Mk IV had production-style electrical units, a modular assembly method and better conditioning and monitoring equipment between the bomb and the aircraft carrying it. It would become available in 1949 and remain in service until 1953, about 550 being built and delivered making the Mk IV the first production-line atom bomb.

In any situation where SAC wanted atom bombs, aircraft would have to fly to one of the National Stockpile Sites. There, the bombs would be assembled, checked out and escorted to the flight line where there were ramps and facilities for uploading the ordnance using a pit for positioning the Mk III or Mk IV into the forward bomb bay of either a B-29 or a B-50. These events would take several days for each squadron. Each bomber would then depart for dispersal bases in Canada, Greenland, England, Guam, or Japan where the strike package would be put together, and flight plans written up. Uploading procedures for the B-36 are covered from page 70.

The US Air Force wanted bigger bombs with higher yields but there was limited availability of fissionable materials, and it was believed that it would be more efficient to build bombs with a yield of 100KT rather than 20KT. Analysis projected that 10 bombs of 20KT yield would each destroy an area of 3.4miles^2 (8.8km^2), a total of 34miles^2 (88km^2). Seven 100KT bombs could be produced with the same amount of fissionable material and each would destroy 10miles^2 (25.9km^2), a net total of 70miles^2 (181.3km^2).

Plutonium from uranum-238 was produced in three reactors at the Hanford Site and the 'Fat Man' implosion bomb required 14lb (6.2kg) of which 21% was fissionable. But deterioration at that location due to decomposition of an initiator (polonium-210) also fell. Uranium-235

BELOW: *The physical destruction of Tokyo provided an analogue for scaling the damage which would be incurred by atomic weapons, a key to calculating the explosive yield required for a given task. USAF*

ABOVE: *Early atomic tests such as Operation Crossroads in 1946 produced data on the blast wave, thermal effects, and destructive potential against a wide range of materials. USAF*

RIGHT: *Initial plans to attack the Soviet Union were compiled in August 1945 using B-29s with limited range compared to the total overlay of national targets provided by the long-range B-36. USAF*

was obtained from enrichment of naturally mined uranium at the Y-12 and K-25 Oak Ridge plants. This was a wasteful process, and a 'Fat Man' bomb was more than 17 times as efficient as the 'Little Boy' type because it makes better use of the neutrons produced by the fission process. But one tonne of uranium ore produced eight times as much U-235 as plutonium, which was up to eight times as expensive to produce as U-235.

With the potential for allowing a 63% increase in the number of available bombs and a 75% increase in yield, the Mk IV went into immediate production from 1949. Manufacture of the Mk III was stopped, the breakthrough had been achieved, and work had already begun on the Mk V bomb weighing little more than 3,000lb (1,360kg) compared to 10,000lb (4,536kg) for the Mk III and predecessors. Further development would get that down to 2,500lb (1,134kg) with selectable yields from 6KT to 100KT. There was now the potential for several hundred bombs and the possibility of that played into the war games and theoretical analyses which would influence revisions to existing war plans.

Under plans in existence in 1948, it was not possible to load an atom bomb into a B-29, fly it across the United States and deliver it to a forward base. But partially assembled bombs could be moved up in that way and that involved a forward-deployed assembly team to take the parts and put them together. As late as April 1950 a classified briefing identified the need for 8,000ft (2,438m) long runways for a B-29 or B-50 to take off carrying an atomic bomb and there were very few places in the world where they were available.

Planners now envisaged 147 bombs dropped on 70 cities with the first hits on D+9. B-29s and B-50s from the UK, Cairo, and Okinawa would carry out the initial atomic attacks and follow through with conventional raids while the B-36s would fly from Alaska. The size and scale of the initial air assault on Russia was now far larger than proposed in earlier war plans, the first wave of a four-phase attack targeting 26 centres of industrial weapons production with 220 bombs on 104 urban centres.

B-29 and B-50 bombers would reach their targets by means of mid-air refuelling with KB-29 tankers. The delivery of atomic bombs would call for 300 bombers covering 6,000 sorties in the initial phase. The B-50s were assigned to hit 51% of targets, the B-29s hitting 35%, the remaining 14%

addressed by the new B-36. The atomic attacks were to be concentrated in the opening days of a war breaking out with the majority of all missions completed in the first 30 days. The B-29s and B-50s would fly out of the UK and this initial phase would last three months with heavy concentration of electronic countermeasures.

Loss Predictions

Integrating Russian air defence elements as known in 1949, the Weapons Systems Evaluation Group assessed the survival of a daylight attack force consisting of 223 B-29s and B-50s carrying 32 atom bombs, concluding that 35 aircraft would be shot down by enemy fighters, two to artillery, five due to technical issues and 14 turning back for various reasons. In all, 24 atom bomb-carriers would reach their assigned targets, three would be shot down, five lost for operational reasons and three completely missing their targets. This produced an aircraft loss rate of 19% and an ordnance delivery rate of 75% on target. The projected loss ratio was twice the average experienced by the Eighth Air Force in World War Two.

For night raids, assuming 96 B-29s and B-50s carrying 32 atom bombs, seven would be shot down by fighters, two brought down by anti-aircraft fire, and two to operational failures. Three bombs would fail to get delivered as

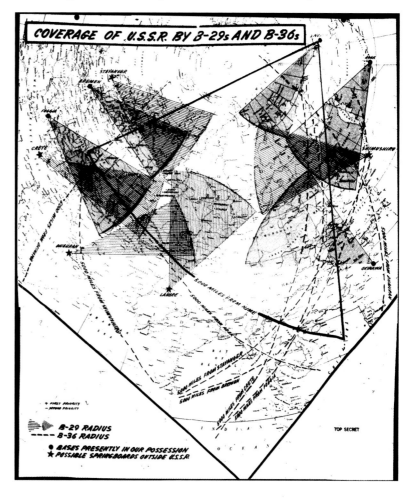

COVERAGE OF U.S.S.R. BY B-29s AND B-36s

B-29 RADIUS
B-36 RADIUS
● BASES PRESENTLY IN OUR POSSESSION
★ POSSIBLE SPRINGBOARDS OUTSIDE U.S.S.R.

TOP SECRET

RUSSIAN & MANCHURIAN STRATEGIC URBAN AREAS

LEFT: *Detailed maps of national resources to be denied to Russia in the event of war defined the size of long-range bomber formations required to do the job. USAF*

planned, four aircraft would be lost due to technical issues and two bombs would miss their planned targets. In this case, losses would be 12% with a 92% bomb-dropping success. But in both cases the loss rates would be totally unacceptable and the attrition rate so high that none of the overall objectives could have been met. SAC would have run out of aircraft, crews, and an ability to sustain the offensive.

Under the revised designation of type classification, in early 1950 SAC had 512 bombers including 337 B-29s and 148 B-50 medium and 27 B-36 heavy bombers. The core aircraft was itself a relative newcomer, the B-29 having only begun to build its reputation when it made its first operational bombing raid on Japan in June 1944, the last aircraft being delivered in May 1946, another victim of post-war contraction and massive defence budget cuts.

Development of the B-29 had been a long and painful process with frequent threats to cancel it as technical

and engineering challenges almost brought it down. Yet, when introduced, it was the most advanced bomber in service anywhere and despite being one of the most complex aircraft built, it bristled with technological innovations and advanced design features. But they had serious problems, the engines frequently overheating, blowing cylinder heads off on starting up, suffering from faulty ignition circuits, leaking oil and poor fuel systems. Under

SAC 1946-1959

The personnel complement and the tactical aircraft inventory of Strategic Air Command 1946-1959 covering the period during which the B-36 served as the primary strategic, long-range bomber.

Year	Officers	Airmen	Civilians	Total personnel	Aircraft
1946	4.319	27,871	4,902	37,092	279
1947	5,175	39,307	5,107	49,589	713
1948	5,562	40,038	6,365	51,965	837
1949	10,050	53,460	7,980	71,490	868
1950	10,600	66,600	8,273	85,473	962
1951	19,747	113,224	11,554	144,525	1,186
1952	20,282	134,072	11,667	166,021	1,638
1953	19,944	138,782	12,256	170,982	1,830
1954	23,447	151,466	14,193	189,106	2,640
1955	26,180	151,595	18,222	195,997	3,068
1956	27,871	169,170	20,238	217,279	3,218
1957	29,946	174,030	20,038	224,014	2,711
1958	34,112	199,562	25,029	258,703	3,031
1959	36,435	199,970	26,204	262,609	3,207

STRATEGIC AIR COMMAND

INFORMATION

The United States' Primary Nuclear Deterrent Force

Peace Is Our Profession

LEFT: *With the expansion of Strategic Air Command during the 1950s, recruiting posters appealed to national patriotism where visitors to air shows were given guides to its function and purpose. SAC*

place the bomb was armed and made live with electrical circuits from a high voltage power source to sequence the release, fusing and detonation of the explosives which would initiate the chain reaction. Safety devices, electrical circuits and plugs ensured the bomb would not detonate prematurely.

The detonators had a shelf life of nine days, giving the weapon its stored duration, while the batteries had to be recharged every 36 hours and cleaned every nine days. Because of thermal heating in the core, it could be left in place for only 10 days to ensure it would not damage the initiators. Several modifications and improvements were made to the refined Mk IV bomb which had an integrated uranium and plutonium pit and later improvements allowed interchangeability of these components to selectively change the yield of the bomb so that it could be 'shaped' for specific targets.

The pit was installed before flight or sometimes during flight facilitated by doors in the nose of the bomb and a port through the casing to allow access to the pit, which was coated in metals to shield the crew from radiation. However, any corrosion would leak harmful radiation to the crew. Changes to the way the detonators were configured offered some safety in preventing unexpected detonation in the event that the carrier-plane crashed. Due to a security scare the name for the conversion programme was changed to Saddletree on May 12, 1947, and aircraft embraced by the modifications now included the B-29, B-50A, and the B-36.

operational conditions, engines had a life of only 270 flying hours before replacement.

The B-29 required considerable rework to adapt them for carrying atom bombs under the 'Silverplate' programme, modifications introduced according to when specific aircraft came through the production cycle and mostly associated with changes to the bomb bay. For these purposes, the B-29 was equipped with the slightly improved R-3350-41 engine which had improved cooling, fuel injection, and an upgraded manifold system. The remotely controlled gun turrets were removed but the tail guns were retained, and the aircraft fitted with reverse-pitch propellers to assist with braking after landing.

The Mk III was the first production atomic bomb carried by the B-29. With plutonium as the core, it was the operational version of 'Fat Man', effectively a live weapon from the time it was assembled, requiring an initiator (the 'urchin') and a shell, all three components being referred to as the 'pit'. With high explosive detonators in

Piston Power for the B-36

How to power the world's biggest bomber was a challenge for Convair, who selected the last in a proud line of Pratt & Witney radial engines

As noted previously, Consolidated wanted a clean and aerodynamically efficient wing for the B-36 and selected a pusher-configuration with leading-edge air inlets for cooling. Tractor-power would incur drag-inducing frontal wing mountings for either radial or in-line engines, their associated cooling scoops being counterproductive to efficient airflow over the wing. With few contenders offering the power required for this aircraft, Consolidated selected the Pratt & Whitney R-4360 engine, at the time a new design but the last of its type this company would produce. However, it was the first from its new plant outside Kansas City, Missouri.

Development of the R-4360 began under the leadership of P&W's Luke Hobbs, taking the company along an unfamiliar path in proposing an air-cooled radial. Options included six rows of six cylinders, three rows of nine cylinders, six rows of five cylinders or five rows of seven cylinders together with several permutations. Hobbs selected four rows of seven cylinders with the same cylinder dimensions as those on the R-2800, but the decision that caused headaches was over the arrangement, in-line or spiral and, if the latter, with a right-handed or left-handed twist. Crucial too was the distance between rows and the impact

that would have on firing sequence and cooling.

Design work began on November 11, 1940, and the first concept engine was running by April 28, 1941. Minimal frontal area was a key selling point to the army and navy customers seeking large powerplants for big aircraft. With war-clouds gathering there was a sense of urgency and as tests evolved, various valve positions were evaluated, the exhaust port initially being placed on top of the cylinder with the intake to the side. Throughout 1941 work accelerated, three complete engines being assembled together with two single-cylinder engines and a single-row, seven-cylinder engine.

BELOW: *Advanced, powerful, and temperamental, the Pratt & Whitney R-4360 was noisy, difficult to maintain and left the B-36 yearning for more power. But it could be made to work well if maintained correctly.*
Via Dennis Jenkins

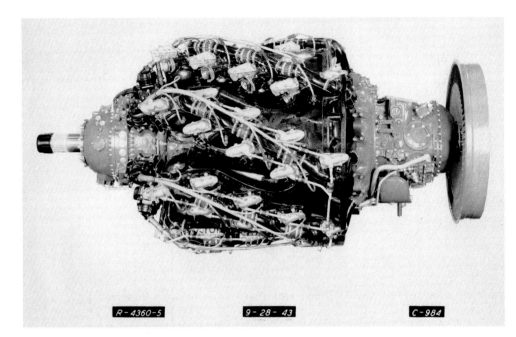

ABOVE: *Hand-crafted and completed on September 28, 1943, the first R-4360 Wasp Major was the only engine in town when Convair went shopping for the most powerful piston-driver around. Via Dennis Jenkins*

It was during this time that P&W's decision to apply forged cylinder heads to all R-2800-C engines rather than cast heads was adopted for the R-4360 as well. This change allowed deeper cooling fins.

The first flight of an R-4360 occurred on May 25, 1942, with the Vultee XA-31A (42-35824), the first RAF Vengeance dive-bomber but adapted for engine tests and re-designated XA-31B. For the next several flights all went well but a ruptured fuel feed diaphragm caused a forced landing in a tobacco field near Hartford, Connecticut, on September 15, 1942. During this year, 10 development engines were delivered for operation with test aircraft and, as interest from aircraft manufacturers increased, the engine had to be shown applicable for tractor or pusher applications and with remote reduction gears and dual rotational propeller configurations. In the case of buried pusher installation, lack of cooling demanded a special fan driven off the rear accessory case, moving those assemblies (starter, generator, and hydraulic pump) to the outer face of the rear case.

The problem of cooling by air coming from different directions ran against convention due to the usual requirement for fin design optimised for flow from either front or rear. Variability too was provided for installation of various types of supercharger, either single-stage, single-speed, variable-speed or two-stage configuration, the change made possible by removing the rear plate and bolting on a supercharger stage. Flexibility in operating mode, either by orientation or location, and in the ability to accommodate different boost requirements held greater promise for airframe manufacturers and their design teams.

On March 1, 1942, P&W assigned military designations to the different

configurations, the first service-engine known as the XR-4360-2 which went to the US Navy (hence the '2' which conformed to the navy tradition of giving their engine model types even numbers). On April 30, type numbers for the various test configurations were assigned and by the end of the year a total of 3,500 test hours had been logged with a total programme expenditure of $5.7m to that date. By this time, the United States was in full wartime mobilisation across the aeronautical industry and throughout the armed services, adding valuable development money funding a major increase in personnel and resources.

Throughout 1943 the testing went on, with variants of the engine demonstrating various power levels and the first production engines being designated R-4360-B to distinguish them from the semi-production lots. By February, the engines for the YB-35 were designated R-4360-21 and the following month those for the B-36 were to be the R-4360-25 type. In June, P&W assigned

the designation R-4360-29 to engines for the proposed XB-44, a single B-29A delivered to P&W as a testbed for the new engine to be introduced with the B-29C, later re-designated B-50A. When the sole example flew it was fitted with the -33 series engines.

Shipment of semi-production engines began in September 1943 for the B-36 test programme with the R-4360-5 going direct to Consolidated, followed a month later by an R-4360-7 for the B-35 programme. Engines continued to be delivered throughout 1944, by the close of which the programme had cost $15.3m, the test time having increased to 12,000 hours with 30 pre-production engines shipped, of which 17 were for the US Army and 13 for the navy. The first full production engine, an R-4360-4, was delivered in January 1945 and a 150-hour type test was completed on February 6.

But the demand for extra performance brought about the B3 configuration, specifically for the B-50A, achieved by reducing the compression ratio from 7.0:1 to 6.7:1 to increase manifold pressure, with cylinder baffles modified to protect the rocker boxes and ignition systems from the heat of the exhaust and strengthened reduction gearing. By the end of 1945, 30 semi-production and 81 production engines had been delivered with total accumulated test time reaching 17,000 hours and a total programme cost of $19.7m.

By this date, the C-series engines were in development, with a rated output of 3,800bhp (2,833kW). By July 1946, the 150-hour model tests for the series 35 engines for the B-50A and the 25-series engines for the B-36 had been completed and it was decided that the B-36 engines should have the C-series features incorporated for a rated thrust of 3,500bhp (2,610kW). This was designated R-3460-41A and by the end of the year total test hours had reached 24,000 and development costs topped $25.7m.

RIGHT: *A briefing to engineers on the Wasp Major as they learn servicing and maintenance requirements which they will convey down the line to field technicians. USAF*

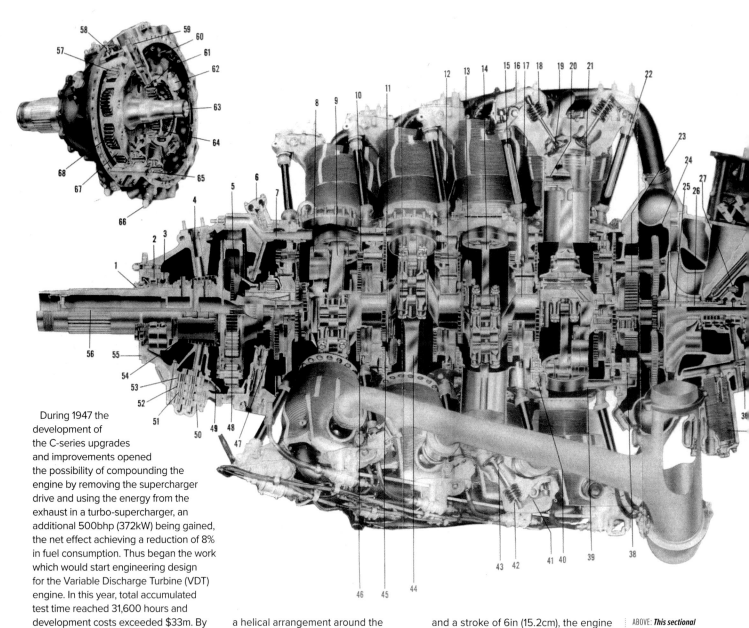

During 1947 the development of the C-series upgrades and improvements opened the possibility of compounding the engine by removing the supercharger drive and using the energy from the exhaust in a turbo-supercharger, an additional 500bhp (372kW) being gained, the net effect achieving a reduction of 8% in fuel consumption. Thus began the work which would start engineering design for the Variable Discharge Turbine (VDT) engine. In this year, total accumulated test time reached 31,600 hours and development costs exceeded $33m. By June 1949, those totals exceeded 40,000 hours and $42.9m, respectively.

By Design

The Wasp Major consisted of 28 cylinders in four rows of seven, with a helical arrangement around the crankcase and each one exposed to the air stream which gave it a better cooling characteristic than other one and two cylinder engines of its time. With a piston displacement of 4,363in³ (71,509cm³), a bore of 5.75in (14.6cm) and a stroke of 6in (15.2cm), the engine had a dry weight of 3,405lb (1,544kg). P&W chose to keep the bore to that size in the belief that they would avoid the problems of detonation experienced later by Wright with the R-3350. The cylinders had forged aluminium

ABOVE: *This sectional illustration of the P&W R-4360 (the 'R' denoting a radial engine) is accompanied by the drive and reduction gear at top left. Pratt & Whitney*

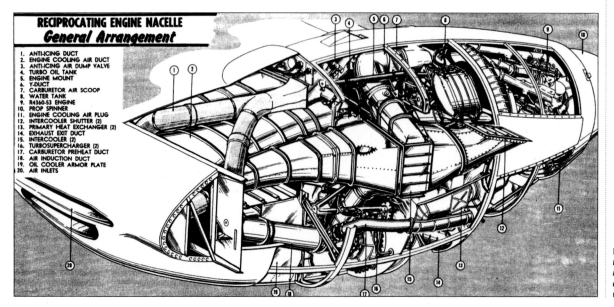

RECIPROCATING ENGINE NACELLE
General Arrangement

1. ANTI-ICING DUCT
2. ENGINE COOLING AIR DUCT
3. ANTI-ICING AIR DUMP VALVE
4. TURBO OIL TANK
5. ENGINE MOUNT
6. Y-DUCT
7. CARBURETOR AIR SCOOP
8. WATER TANK
9. R4360-53 ENGINE
10. PROP SPINNER
11. ENGINE COOLING AIR PLUG
12. INTERCOOLER SHUTTER (2)
13. PRIMARY HEAT EXCHANGER (2)
14. EXHAUST EXIT DUCT
15. INTERCOOLER (2)
16. TURBOSUPERCHARGER (2)
17. CARBURETOR PREHEAT DUCT
18. AIR INDUCTION DUCT
19. OIL COOLER ARMOR PLATE
20. AIR INLETS

LEFT: *The R-4360 turbo-supercharger and intercooler packaged into a compact area within the wing section. Convair*

1. Propeller Shaft Thrust Nut
2. Propeller Shaft Roller Bearing
3. Propeller Shaft Ball Bearing
4. Governor Drive Shaftgear
5. Propeller Shaft Reduction Drive Gear Outer Coupling
6. Spark Advance Control Valve
7. Crankcase Pressure Oil Line
8. Crankshaft Front Counterweight
9. D Row Masterod Assembly
10. Cam Small Drive Shaftgear
11. Cam Large Drive Shaftgear
12. Crankshaft Center Main Bearing
13. Crankshaft Oil Slinger
14. B Row Linkrod
15. Inlet Valve Pushrod
16. Inlet Valve Rocker
17. Crankshaft
18. Inlet Valve Springs
19. Inlet Valve
20. Pistonpin
21. Piston and Rings
22. Pushrod Cover
23. Impeller Drive Damper
24. Impeller Intermediate Drive
25. Impeller and Shaft Assembly
26. Accessory Drive Shaft
27. Impeller Shaft Rear Rings Breather
28. Fuel Feed Valve
29. Tachometer Drive Shaftgear
30. Fuel Pump Drive Shaftgear
31. Fuel Pump Intermediate Drive
32. Rear Oil Distributor Ring
33. Starter Drive Shaftgear
34. Generator or Accessory Drive Shaftgear
35. Rear Accessory Drive Gear
36. Rear Accessory Drive Oil Pressure Reducing Valve
37. Pressure Oil Strainer
38. Collector Case Oil Pump
39. Crankcase Scavenge Oil Line
40. Crankcase Scavenge Oil Pump
41. Exhaust Valve Rocker
42. Exhaust Valve Springs
43. Exhaust Valve
44. C Row Masterod
45. Cam Drive Gear
46. Cam
47. Magneto Intermediate Drive Gear
48. Propeller Shaft Reduction Drive Gear
49. Front Accessory Drive Gear
50. Torquemeter Pump
51. Front Power Section Scavenge Pump
52. Rocker Drain Scavenge Pump
53. Front Section Scavenge Pump
54. Propeller Shaft Oil Transfer Bearing
55. Thrust Cover
56. Propeller Oil Feed Tube
57. Propeller Shaft Reduction Drive Fixed Gear
58. Torquemeter Oil Pressure Transmitter
59. Magneto Drive Shaft
60. Spark Advance Oil Feed Tube
61. Magneto Drive Fixed Gear
62. Spark Advance Cylinder
63. Propeller Shaft
64. Magneto Drive Shaftgear
65. Torquemeter Master Piston
66. Torquemeter Oil Pressure Relief Valve
67. Propeller Shaft Reduction Pinion Support
68. Propeller Shaft Reduction Pinion

heads and deep-cut cooling fins and an integral valve housing which was screwed and shrunk on to a forged-steel cylinder barrel.

The full skirt and forged aluminium pistons each had three compression rings, a single dual oil control ring and an oil scraper ring with the top compression ring chromium plated on the face which bore against the cylinder wall. The one-piece crankshaft was in forged steel with four throws and supported in the crankcase by five, steel-backed main bearings with the weights of the reciprocating elements connected to the crankpin and counterbalanced by fixed and bifilar (two parallel threaded) counterweights. The propeller shaft was supported at the crankshaft end by a plain lead-bronze bearing and at the propeller end by a roller-bearing, which carried the radial loads, and a deep-groove ball bearing for absorbing thrust loads.

A four-barrel pressure-type Stromberg carburettor provided automatic mixture control feeding metered fuel through internal passages thrown centrifugally through orifices between impeller blades to mix with combustion air. The mixture passed through the diffuser to the blower rim and to the cylinders via seven intake pipes for each bank of four cylinders. Two types of boost were available, either a single-stage, single-speed supercharger integrated with an exhaust driven turbo-supercharger or a single-stage, hydraulically driven, variable-speed supercharger.

Ignition included seven Scintilla shielded magnetos with integral distributor in each one which operated at half the speed of the crankshaft, each magneto providing dual ignition for the bank of four cylinders directly above. The planetary spur reduction gears were of the Pratt & Whitney type with optional ratios. Lubrication was provided by force-feed, gear-type oil pumps to all parts of the engine and all accessory drive gears were driven by a bevel gear revolving at crankshaft speed.

Chasing Power

Pratt & Whitney faced a unique challenge in determining the best firing sequence for multi-row radials. No one before or since has manufactured a production-line radial engine with more than two cylinder rows. In the R-4360, even firing would produce a cylinder ignition every 25.714285°, the product of 720 divided by the 28 cylinders. In the configuration with seven cylinders in a row, each is displaced 51.4288571° to its neighbour. The staggered offset is determined by dividing 25.714285 by two (12.857142), which produces the spiral shape of the four seven-cylinder rows.

That also dictates even firing by considering each bank to be a four-cylinder, in-line engine, in which the convention is to have pistons moving in pairs; the two outer cylinders followed by the two middle cylinders in unison. The sequence was different with the R-4360 in that, as viewed from the front, individual cylinders in rows one and three would operate together at the same time as equivalent cylinders in rows two and four. Dynamically, this balances the operation of the R-4360 as seven, four-cylinder engines to produce an even firing sequence.

In the event of a failed magneto, one bank of four cylinders would be taken out and thus avoid disrupting the balanced stress load and preventing unacceptable vibration. Conversely, automobile engines can accept a higher level of vibration, and many were designed without even-number firing. Chrysler's V-10 is one example, which has a 90° included angle rather than the favoured 70° angle which works because it is two V-8 blocks with two additional cylinders attached. To make this operate effectively, pairs of cylinders are fired on opposing banks

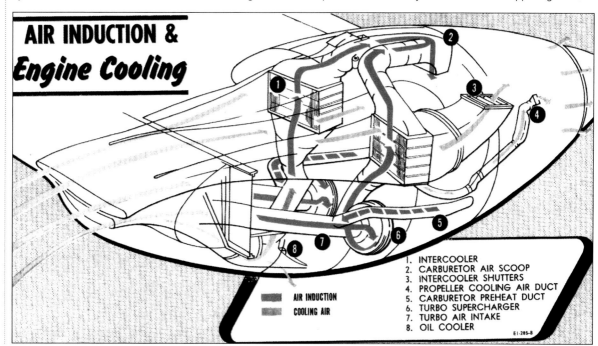

RIGHT: The air induction and cooling system wrapped beneath the anti-icing duct. Convair

AIR INDUCTION & Engine Cooling

■ AIR INDUCTION
■ COOLING AIR

1. INTERCOOLER
2. CARBURETOR AIR SCOOP
3. INTERCOOLER SHUTTERS
4. PROPELLER COOLING AIR DUCT
5. CARBURETOR PREHEAT DUCT
6. TURBO SUPERCHARGER
7. TURBO AIR INTAKE
8. OIL COOLER

E1-205-B

one VDT engine replacing the R-4360 on the starboard inner position. It was considered the prototype for the B-54A and designated as such on May 29, 1948, along with an order for 33, production of which would carry the enhanced engine delivering 4,500bhp (3,355kW). The B-54 was never adopted, and no airframe was completed.

As early as March 1947 Convair had proposed that 34 of the 100 B-36s on order be fitted with VDT engines but the Pratt & Whitney R-4360 VDT had to drive tractor, rather than pusher, propellers which meant the wing having to support a 10ft (3m) shaft extending through the entire wing chord. That required redesign of the trailing edge flaps and the internal cooling system as

which suffers only in the undesirable exhaust note it produces!

In seeking further advances and increased output, P&W embarked on a radical development of the R-4360 based on a turbo-supercharger and direct fuel injection. Power would be regulated by clamshell doors on the discharge side which, when closed off, would restrict the flow of exhaust gases, and slow the rotation rate of the turbine. In turn, this would slow the compressor and reduce the mass flow to the engine. The fuel injector control unit would regulate the flow of fuel proportional to the mass air flow. For increased power, the clamshell doors would open, the exhaust gas flow would increase and provide additional power to the turbine and from there to the compressor.

Major challenges with the clamshell doors were encountered and with the design of a variable discharge nozzle but the promise of an added output was tempting. Some engineers proposed injecting unburned fuel into the exhaust, producing an 'afterburner' effect which necessitated large aftercoolers to keep temperatures within acceptable levels on the discharge side of the compressor. In examining ways to boost rated power, a wide range of options were considered and 0.25:1 scale models were built and tested for turbo-compound derivatives, some even strapped two turbo-superchargers in parallel to boost power and all came under the generic title of Variable Discharge Turbines (VDTs).

P&W was in overall control of the VDT programme but relied heavily on General Electric for the modified turbo-supercharger control units and when tests were conducted in a modified B-50 the operation had to be controlled manually. With all the uncertainty of a turbo running away with catastrophic results, in theory the VDT was a sound concept and promised much; in practice, as with so much in engineering, it was fraught with problems and technical challenges. When it began to operate the B-50, the US Air Force wanted it, and the B-36, to get the VDT engines and it ordered one aircraft, designated YB-50C, to be modified for trials as precursor to the B-54, essentially a B-50 (46-061) with

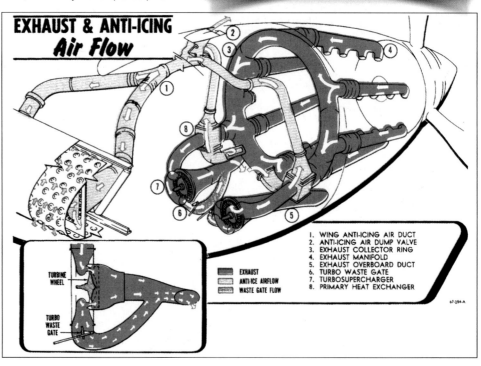

EXHAUST & ANTI-ICING
Air Flow

1. WING ANTI-ICING AIR DUCT
2. ANTI-ICING AIR DUMP VALVE
3. EXHAUST COLLECTOR RING
4. EXHAUST MANIFOLD
5. EXHAUST OVERBOARD DUCT
6. TURBO WASTE GATE
7. TURBOSUPERCHARGER
8. PRIMARY HEAT EXCHANGER

EXHAUST
ANTI-ICE AIRFLOW
WASTE GATE FLOW

TURBINE WHEEL

TURBO WASTE GATE

well as changes to the forward fuselage to resist vibrations. It was believed that VDT engines would boost top speed to 410mph (660kph), provide the aircraft with a 45,000ft (13,716m) service ceiling and retain the same range and bomb load. Convair funded airframe modifications for one aircraft by deleting three B-36s from the original contract, approved by the air force in July 1947.

After a year-long analysis and significant engineering study, Convair discovered that the cruising speed over a range of 7,250 miles (11,665km) was 262mph (421kph), some 23mph (37kph) slower than existing aircraft. Five VDT aircraft designated B-36C (44-92099 to 44-92103) had been cut out of the production order to compensate for cost inflation and to pay for the new project.

Pratt &Whitney built more than 363,000 engines during the war and by 1946 had reconverted all manufacturing to its home facility at East Hartford, Connecticut to produce six different models, including three versions of the R-4360 Wasp Major, capable of delivering more than 3,500bhp (2,609kW). There was enthusiasm for further development of the Wasp Major, at the time the most powerful engine in production, and

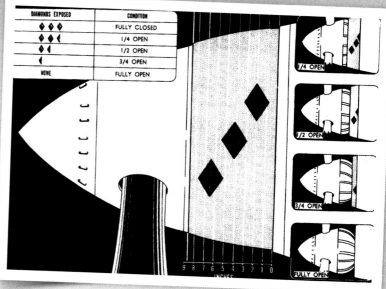

DIAMONDS EXPOSED	CONDITION
◆ ◆ ◆	FULLY CLOSED
◆ ◆ ◀	1/4 OPEN
◆ ◀	1/2 OPEN
◀	3/4 OPEN
NONE	FULLY OPEN

engineers believed that it was far short of its ultimate potential.

At the end of the war, some contraction occurred as well as consolidation around manufacturing facilities, and in addition to the B-36 and the B-50, the Wasp Major powered the Douglas C-74 Globemaster and the Martin BTM Mauler. The Boeing 377 Stratocruiser would also be powered by the R-4360 in addition to the unsuccessful Republic Rainbow, the Douglas XC-112, the Goodyear F2G Corsair, and the Republic XF-12. By the end of the decade, the Wasp Major powered more USAF multi-engine aircraft than any other engine, including the C-97, C-119, and C-124A transport aircraft and the US Navy's Martin Mercator maritime patrol aircraft.

As the company neared its 25th anniversary, the chief engineer at Pratt & Whitney and one of the great engine design and development engineers at the company, Andy Willgoos, passed away. He died on March 1, 1949, a day before a B-50 powered by the Wasp Major completed a round-the-world flight of 94hr 1min. He was remembered through the Andrew Willgoos Turbine Laboratory, a windowless, six-storey steel and concrete structure on the east bank of the Connecticut River only a short distance away from the main plant. In those test cells it was possible

to simulate environmental conditions from sea-level to more than 70,000ft (21,336m). By 1949 it was primarily working the development of gas turbine engines supported by the paraphernalia associated with reaction propulsion systems. It was demolished in 2012.

A total of 18,696 R-4360 engines were produced.

Relevant to the story of engines for US bombers, mention must be made of the Lycoming XR-7755, the largest piston-engine built in the United States and exceeded only by the Yakovlev M-501 diesel engine which formed the basis for the later family of Zvezda M503 marine engines. The XLR-7755 was specifically designed with an eye on the requirement for a heavy bomber which later matured into the B-36 programme.

The 36-cylinder, four-row, liquid-cooled radial had a displacement of 7,756in³ (127,120cm³) and an output of 5,000bhp (2,378kW). The massive engine had a length of 10ft (3m) and a diameter of 5ft (1.5m) with a weight of 6,050lb (2,744kg). Development began in 1943 under the guidance of Clarence Wiegman and tests began in 1944. It was cancelled two years later for lack of an application in the rapid replacement of reciprocating engines with the gas turbine for fighter and bomber development.

Prop Variants

From prototypes to initial variants, when the B-36 entered SAC, it brought a new era in strategic bombing assets but struggled to achieve the desired performance.

Long awaited by advocates pushing for an intercontinental strategic bomber, essential as a deterrent, and required for a potential war with the Soviet Union, the first XB-36 (42-13570) was rolled out on September 8, 1945, less than a week after the end of World War Two which was marked by the Japanese surrender. Aircraft weight was up and projected performance down from the requirements set by the Army Air Corps and anticipated by the AAF from 1941. Delays caused by the general war production of existing bombers made it later than had been hoped for, but there were flaws too in the aircraft as it emerged from the Fort Worth factory.

Materials provided by contractors were found to contain imperfections resulting from disruptive action by labour unions at the Aluminum Corporation of America (ALCOA) which provided Convair with most of its metal.

This played back into the general condition of the first XB-36, which was judged unsuitable for anything other than as an aerodynamic test vehicle for early flights. And on April 27, 1945, a decision had been made to prepare the second prototype (42-13571) closer to production standard than was originally intended, re-designating it as the YB-36. It was the first of the series to roll out of Building 4 at Government Plant No 4.

Significant changes had been made to the defensive armament, the original design incorporating a gunner in each of the upper and lower forward and upper and lower aft fuselage turrets, each with two sighting blisters, and a tail position operated by a gunner in the aft crew compartment. In 1944 this had been changed to eight retractable turrets in four pairs above and below the fuselage and with a single tail position. When the APG-7 Eagle radar was replaced by the AN/APG-3 from the B-29 programme in

March 1945, the paired lower forward fuselage turrets were removed, the forward defensive arc covered by an additional nose gun position.

About 7,000 Convair employees watched as the XB-36 took to the air for the first time shortly after 10am on August 8, 1946, piloted by Beryl A Erickson and G S 'Gus' Green, with flight engineers J D McEachern and William 'Bill' P Easley, flight test engineer Robert E Hewes, flight test analysts W H Vobbe and A W Gedeman, and observers W I Daniel and Joe M. Hefley. In a relatively uneventful flight lasting 37 minutes in which the undercarriage remained down, and a flap failed to retract, the heaviest aircraft ever to take to the air performed as expected. The flight was conducted at 3,500ft (1,067m) and a speed of 155mph (249kph) over the downtown area of Fort Worth with a throbbing reverberation that many people around

ABOVE: *The XB-36 with original nose glazing and cockpit arrangement which would change dramatically for the initial production series and be subject to continuous modification.* Via Dennis Jenkins

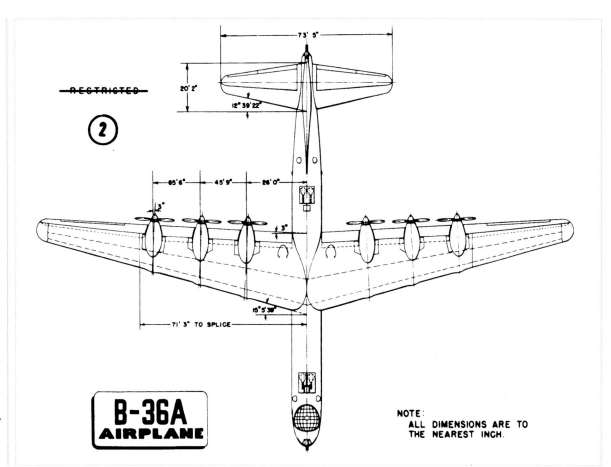

RIGHT: *The planform of the B-36A and B, initial variants with the air force showing the 15.12° leading edge wing sweep.* Convair

BELOW: *Dimensions of the B-36A and B variants with the wide centre-of-gravity limits between 23.5% and 45% of the mean aerodynamic chord.* Convair

NOTE:
ALL DIMENSIONS ARE TO THE NEAREST INCH.

B-36A
AIRPLANE

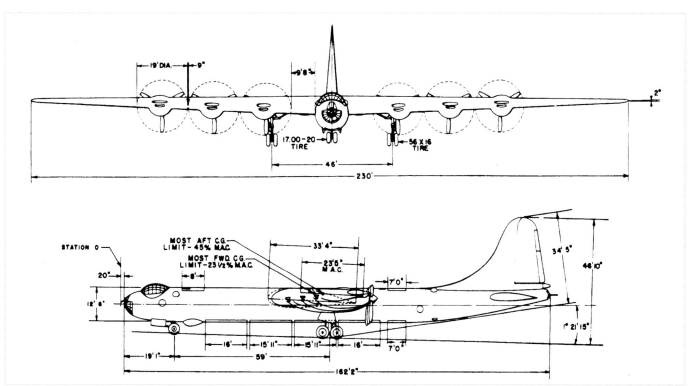

the world would come to know as the unmistakable sound of six Wasp Majors.

In the following flights and in the early test phase it was apparent that the aircraft was low on performance, plagued with persistent engine problems and dangerous propeller vibrations. A new propeller would be introduced but not before one shattered during a test flight attracting negative

comments from the technical press. Reassuringly, the aircraft had poor stall characteristics in wind tunnels which proved not to be the case during trials in the air. And when a trailing airspeed indicator and cable broke loose from an aircraft in flight, sending it crashing through the toilet of a school, a local press report noted that the bomber had found its first target!

Regarded as a qualification test-bed for improvements and for training purposes, the XB-36 flew in June 1948 with its new four-wheel bogie main gear and was handed over to SAC as a training airframe devoid now of flight test equipment. It was soon back at Fort Worth, the YB-36 (42-13571) having made its first flight on December 4, 1947, where it conducted special

over as the aircraft had to be tipped tail down so that the vertical fin could clear the exit.

A potentially major manufacturing challenge was the use of magnesium panels, engineered in primarily secondary structures introducing problems with quality bonding. Some areas used Metlbond, specially developed by Convair for this aircraft and found to be useful in areas where vibration affected flight structures and in places where rivet joints were stressed in conventional airframes. The greatest challenge was to integrate corrective solutions into a unified production upgrade added to the daunting task of manufacturing or procuring oversize components; the only place where the massive main landing gear struts could be manufactured was at the US Naval Gun Factory!

B-36A

The first production version of the B-36 lacked many systems required by the specification and for effective operation as a strategic bomber. Only 22 were built (44-92004 to 44-92025). Similar to the YB-36, the B-36A had six R-4350-25 Wasp engines but initially without any defensive armament, only the tail turret being added later to this variant. With no war load and with full tanks it could be ferried over a

tests, including one flight with the experimental tracked main landing gear, applying a force of only 57psi (383kPa) to the runway compared with 156psi (1,075kPa) with the four-wheel bogie arrangement.

With new engines, new landing gear, and a rigorous test programme, improvements and upgrades introducing production-level standards and better performance, the YB-36 was delivered to the US Air Force as a B-36A on May 31, 1949. It returned to Fort Worth for conversion to a RB-36E configuration and as a reference standard for that variant, the first B-36A having been subject to destructive testing. It was retired in 1957 and scrapped, some parts ending up on a farm in Newbury, Ohio, owned by Walter Soplata.

Assembling a B-36 took place in separate areas of the main fabrication facility at Fort Worth. The major components section received parts from other places and offsite subcontractors and took up about one-third of the south end of the facility. The major mating section brought in separate wing sections where they were joined together and attached to the fuselage centre-section and bomb bays. The final assembly section incorporated 11 substations to progressively complete the aircraft up the line, receiving landing gear, wing leading and trailing edge sections, internal systems, and subsystems, six engine nacelles and completed wiring, pneumatics, and hydraulics.

In parallel, engine build-up began with the Wasps received from Pratt & Whitney in crates, unpacked and suspended on a six-point overhead rack assembly where they received ancillary equipment, the engine manufacturer working closely with Convair technicians to better understand subtle changes which could improve integration with the airframes. Turbochargers were added

along with electrical wiring and final assembly completed, units hung on their mountings and cowls attached.

Because as fully completed the aircraft could not fit inside the 200ft (60.96m) wide main assembly building, when the wing outer sections and tips were attached at the eighth assembly station the aircraft, now with a full 230ft (70.1m) span, was slewed to a diagonal angle from which point it crabbed down the line. And its indignity was still not

ABOVE: *The flight engineer's console with its six throttle levers.*
Via Dennis Jenkins

BELOW: *Maintenance personnel get to know B-36A 44-9212 at Carswell AFB.*
Via Dennis Jenkins

with limitations on the undercarriage, maximum take-off weight was 310,380lb (140,788kg). Ironically, the first B-36A beat the YB-36 into the air by several months but from the outset this was used for publicity and took pride of place at several public events both at Fort Worth and at nearby Carswell AFB where it was displayed to full public view.

Its future lay in its use as a destructive test frame for structural loads analysis and for that latter purpose it made two flights, one of which lasted seven hours 36 minutes around the pattern at Fort Worth before carrying only enough equipment for a ferry flight to Wright Field at the hands of Colonel Thomas P Gerrity and Convair's chief test pilot Beryl Erickson. It was delivered to Air Materiel Command in May 1948 on its second and last flight, the Air Proving Ground Command at Eglin AFB receiving the aircraft for climate tests on June 18, 1948.

Before delivery, significant progress was made getting the B-36A into a fit state for delivery. On April 8-9, 44-92013 completed a demonstration flight lasting 33 hours 10 minutes covering 6,922 miles (11,137km) in a continuous loop between Fort Worth and San Diego. Simulating an operational flight, the aircraft was loaded with ballast to compensate for the lack of armament and dummy 500lb (226.8kg) bombs were dropped from 21,000ft (6,400m) over the air force bombing range at Wilcox, Arizona. Halfway through the flight two engines gave trouble, cutting the average speed to a lowly 214mph (344kph).

distance of 9,136 miles (14,700km), an unprecedented performance but the general enthusiasm displayed by the US Air Force to news media, especially the aviation press, had one eye on its deterrent factor as much as its applicability to real war situations. The B-36A was far from an effective tool for conflict and was a poor shadow of what later variants would become.

Assigned crew numbered 15 personnel, but eight of these were gunners who in this initial production model had no armament, the remaining crew members being the two pilots, the radar-bombardier, navigator, fight engineer, and two radio men. For most of the time the crew had their hands full as the performance and lack of reliability haunted the B-36 programme in these early days of operational trials and testing in an active environment.

The first B-36A (44-92004) took to the air for the first time on August 28, 1947, ahead of the first YB-36, carrying the new four-wheel bogie arrangement but,

airframe being rebuilt into a RB-36E and delivered as such in July 1951.

B-36B

Regarded as the first variant considered operationally capable of conducting SAC mission requirements, the B-36B was a considerable improvement over its predecessor. With more powerful and efficient R-460-41 engines it had improved electronics including the AN/APQ-24 bombing navigation radar to replace the APG-23A in the B-36A, and it could carry an 86,000lb (39,009kg) bomb load, 14,000lb (6,350kg) more than its predecessor. Of greater strategic importance, it could carry

ABOVE: B-36A 44-92014 on a 'get-to-know-you' open day which did much to project the new image of the recently independent US Air Force. Via Dennis Jenkins

LEFT: B-36B 44-92057 during assembly, displaying respective skin textures from different metals. Via Dennis Jenkins

The same aircraft made another simulated long-range flight on May 13-14, 1948, at a gross weight of 299,619lb (135,907kg), remaining airborne for 36 hours eight minutes covering 8,062 miles (12,972km). Carrying 10,000lb (4,536kg) of dummy bombs and a ballast of 5,796lb (2,629kg) simulating defensive armament, it flew a profile close to that envisaged for an operational strike. The first 369 miles (593.7km) were at 5,000ft (1,524m) followed by a power climb to 10,000ft (4,048m) for a further 30 minutes when the aircraft climbed to 25,000ft (7,620m) for a maximum speed bombing run incorporating 17 minutes of evasive manoeuvres and a return to base at the same altitude.

In further flight proving trials, on May 18 another B-36A dropped 25 2,000lb (907kg) bombs from an altitude of 31,000ft (9,449m) across the Naval Range at Corpus Christi, Texas, part

way on a 7,000 mile (11,263km) flight. A maximum capacity bomb load of 72,000lb (32,659kg) was dropped during a flight on June 30, 1948, by far the greatest weight of bombs dropped by a single aircraft and a record that would stand for a long time.

The first B-36A delivered to an operational unit, 44-92015 arrived at the 7th BW at Carswell AFB on June 26, 1948, having taxied over the perimeter at Fort Worth. On board was Amon G Carter carrying a plaque bearing the name *City of Fort Worth*. The aircraft was assigned to the 492nd Bomb Squadron (BS). Only eight months later the last of 22 B-36As was delivered, 20 of the total production lot serving with the 7th BW at Carswell for training and familiarisation as well as additional flight testing. But their reliability was poor, the readiness level fell far below 50% and the operational life was short, the last

atomic bombs weighing up to 43,000lb (19,504kg) while 18 of this variant could handle the remotely-controlled VB-13 Tarzon bombs, two per aircraft. A total of 62 B-36Bs were accepted, a further four being converted to B-36Ds prior to acceptance and seven delivered as RB-36Ds (see page 88).

The first B-36B (44-92026) made its initial flight on July 8, 1948, when Beryl Erickson took it into the air at Fort Worth. It was accepted by the air force on November 25, 1948 and assigned to the 7th BW at Carswell AFB, joining the B-36As in their training role. It would be used for propeller tests and was converted to a B-6D configuration. The 11th BW also stood up with the B-36B, the first of its aircraft (44-92050) delivered on March 18, 1949, for the 98th BS but was destroyed in an accident on April 15, 1952, with the loss of 15 of a crew of 17.

With a full suite of operational equipment, the B-36B had the advantage of the 3,500hp (2,608kW) R-4360-41 engine which had water injection, but this came at the price of substantial modifications to the structure of the wing which served as a template for retrofit to some of the A-series aircraft. In addition, the 16 20mm cannon were installed in all eight turrets, including the six retractable turrets in the fuselage, and the nose and tail turrets. The tail turret was directed using the AN/APG-3 gun-laying radar and a periscope gunsight was mounted in the bombardier's station. The B-36 also incorporated armoured panels to protect the outer wing fuel tanks. Because the inner tanks were empty by the time the aircraft reached hostile air space, the inboard tanks were left unarmoured to save weight.

Convair had planned to equip the B-36B with the Farrand Y-1 retractable periscope bombsight, but the Norden M-9 sight was used when delays brought about by development problems rendered them unavailable for production. Eventually, the Y-1 was retrofitted to some B types, as evidenced by a flat, glazed nose section. The normal crew complement

of 15 retained the same positions as those in the B-36A, the eight gunners including three for forward and five for aft turrets. Invariably, problems with the defensive armament left little time to address potential targets, as much of the time was devoted to sorting out mechanical and electrical problems with the guns and the radar on the B-36B.

Arguably lacking in sensitivity but militarily significant and a message to politicians still uncertain about the aircraft's worth, on December 7-8, 1948, the seventh anniversary of the Japanese attack on Pearl Harbor, a B-36B got into Hawaiian air space undetected and dropped a 10,000lb (4,536kg) bomb load in the ocean a short

distance away. Three months later, in March 1949, a B-36B dropped 10,000lb (4,536kg) of bombs after an 8,400 mile (13,515km) flight from Fort Worth to Honolulu. But these were the first of some extraordinary demonstration and test flights conducted to evaluate and to display the aircraft's operational capabilities.

On January 19, 1949, a B-36B dropped two 43,000lb (19,505kg) bombs on Muroc Dry Lake, California, the first from a height of 35,000ft (10,668m), the second from 41,000ft (12,497m). The next day B-36A 44-92023 dropped 72 1,000lb (454kg) bombs following a series of tests dropping loads of 31 bombs from varying

altitudes. By mid-October, a B-36 had demonstrated an 8,000 mile (12,872km) flight dropping 25,000lb (11,340kg) of bombs en route.

Opinions varied as to the aircraft's true value to SAC, but Curtis LeMay was insistent that the B-36 should be the aircraft of choice for its long reach into potential enemy airspace, criticising a proposed Boeing B-54 of which 43 in bomber and reconnaissance variants had been ordered on May 29, 1948. Essentially a developed version of the B-50 but with R-4360-51 VDT engines, the B-54 was cancelled on April 18, 1949, following urgent lobbying from SAC. In a direct intervention, LeMay argued that while the B-36 required more apron space, that was not a problem and that initial reports on servicing the aircraft were favourable.

But there were cancellation threats from elsewhere too when the US Navy contested the role of the US Air Force for the strategic atomic deterrent, and specifically over the cost and vulnerability of the B-36. In early 1949 anonymous claims of corruption and poor performance of the B-36 were made prompting Congressional hearings in which these claims were proven to be false. In October, further hearings debated the role of the air force and the navy in the nation's defence which concluded that SAC held that primary role and the B-36 was the correct choice.

There were certainly operational difficulties with the aircraft, the more powerful engines for the B-36B requiring additional fuel tanks in a bomb bay which frequently leaked, and the new defensive armament had technical issues which were never fully corrected before the type was retired. Throughout, the air force kept up an impressive display of its performance to allay fears in political circles and raise the public profile of this giant bomber, which never

failed to impress wherever it appeared on public display.

To sustain that image, on March 10, 1949, a B-36B from the 7th BW/492nd BS, departed from Carswell AFB and flew 9,600 miles (15,446km) in a flight lasting 43 hours 37 minutes by way of Minneapolis, across to Great Falls and on to Key West. Dropping 10,000lb (4,536kg) of bombs into the Gulf of Mexico, it turned northwest over Fort Worth, back across to Great Falls and on to Spokane before landing at Fort Worth after two engines failed. Ordered down due to inclement weather, it had sufficient reserve to have made a 10,000 mile (16,090km) flight with a 10,000lb (4,536kg) bomb load, thus matching the 10x10 requirement set in its original specification.

As the programme got into its stride, more bases would be needed, construction having already been underway since 1947 at Limestone, Maine, with plans for other B-36 groups to form up at Rapid City, South Dakota, and Fairfield-Suisun, California. It was readily apparent that even with its great range, the B-36 could not cover all potential targets from existing and presently planned bases. Accordingly,

several pre-strike staging bases were set up in the far north of the United States from where overflights of the North Pole could be mounted to penetrate deep into the Soviet Union.

There was a difficulty with this as the magnetic compasses were unreliable at extreme northerly latitudes, prompting development of the GEM programme (Global Electronics Modification). The B-36 was already introducing a new way of dispersing and supporting strategic bombing missions and with GEM the 7th BW was able to move to bases in Goose Bay, Labrador, Limestone and Eielson Field close to Fairbanks, Alaska. Because of the potential need to rescue aircraft from extreme latitudes and to search for aircraft in snow and ice, the wing tips and tails of these aircraft were painted bright red for visual detection.

But there were problems with this. The intercontinental range of the aircraft belied its ability to perform as required in war. Reliability was rock bottom, with only seven or eight aircraft out of the 40 on hand during 1949 considered capable of carrying out operations. The 7th BW was very much a test unit, but the poor experience was, in reality, very little different to the integration

ABOVE: *Convair B-36B 44-29033 of the 7th BW showing its clean lines and Arctic recognition colours. Vie Dennis Jenkins*

BELOW: *A varied mix of B-36A and B variants with orange Arctic identification colours. Via Dennis Jenkins*

continued to prove troublesome, the migration into the greater complexity of equipment that had worked well on the B-29 paying a price for its sophistication with frequent breakdowns and ineffective operation. Of particular concern was the AN/APG-3 gun-laying tail radar, frequent failure bringing caustic comments from the most senior levels in the Eighth AF. But not all these failures were technical. By the end of 1950, three aircraft from Carswell had crashed with the loss of 12 airmen. On September 15, 1949, B-36B 44-92079 from the 7th BW was the first hull lost when it crashed into Lake Worth right at the end of the runway, five crewmembers of the 13 on board losing their lives.

A potentially more destructive event occurred five months later. On February 13, 1950, B-36B 44-92075

piloted by Captain Harold L Barry and 16 crewmembers departed Eielson AFB, Alaska, on a training flight down to San Francisco where it would simulate dropping an atom bomb before landing at Carswell AFB, Texas. During appalling weather, in the early hours of the morning the aircraft iced up and three engines caught fire at 15,000ft (3,658m). Capt Barry dropped the bomb, a Mk IV but without a core, which fell into the Pacific Ocean, its implosion charges detonating at a height of 3,000ft (914m) causing a bright flash as the 5,000lb (2,268kg) of high explosive detonated. The crew baled out, but five died and the aircraft crashed on Vancouver Island in northern British Columbia.

Following a request for suggestions from Convair employees, On April 14, 1949, the B-36 was given the name 'Peacemaker' which fitted with Strategic

history of previous aircraft, compounded many said due to the complexity of the aircraft itself and by the legacy of concurrency. Aircraft frequently had to be cannibalised to provide parts that failed to turn up when required, or for equipment that needed replacement or to be returned-to-sender for repair, refurbishment, or replacement.

Moreover, the APQ-24 radar failed to live up to performance during service testing. The defensive armament

Air Command's motto of 'Peace is our Profession'. Notwithstanding complaints from several sectors of the general public, including the clergy one of whom challenged the use of that name in that, as he claimed, it invoked the real peacemaker, who was "not built by Consolidated", the name was never officially adopted, and became the moniker that has been applied by enthusiasts, advertisers, and the pro-defence orientated media ever since.

Still the aircraft was prone to mishaps and technical failure, on occasions causing a cascade of malfunctions resulting in a total loss of the aircraft. In one incident on November 22, 1950, a B-36B (44-92035) was returning to Carswell AFB after firing its guns over the Matagorda Island range. On the way to the range the No.1 engine lost an alternator and flames triggered a suppressant, shutting it down while the pilots feathered the propeller. Over the range the 20mm cannon was fired accompanied immediately by a fire in the APQ-24 radar causing that to shut down and the liaison transmitter to fail.

With the possibility that the gun vibrations had short-circuited internal radar components, the aircraft turned for home before the No.3 engine also failed, prompting the pilot to divert to Kelly AFB, San Antonio, only to discover

that all the electrical circuits for the engines had been lost too. When the bombardier attempted to jettison the bombs, he discovered that the doors would not open and as weather closed in the aircraft was diverted from Kelly to Bergstrom AFB, Texas, but the weather there too caused a further diversion to Carswell AFB. With a mere 21 miles (34km) to go, the No.5 engine died, and the crew baled out, one man being killed when he struck the No.3 propeller and a second dying when his parachute failed.

Technical failures were common, and much was being learned in the

process about an aircraft complex to operate yet consistently used to trial new electronic and system hardware. The inertia in technology development, especially in avionics and both offensive and defensive systems put stress on the crew and on the operational demands of individual combat units. The international situation had created concern that SAC may have to go to war prematurely and before it had completely mastered the way of operating this demanding aircraft. With the Berlin blockade and the detonation of a Soviet atom bomb in August 1949, global tensions were increasing, and the Chinese revolution of that same month brought the world's most populous nation under communist rule.

These factors weighed hard as SAC struggled with operational requirements to support the B-36, persistent moves to reduce the US defence budget threatening its development and, some would say, a portent for outright cancellation. Committed to a balanced economy and paying back the war debt, President Truman froze the US defence budget at $11bn for 1949, a financial year starting July 1, 1948. The US Air Force wanted to increase the number of combat groups from 59 to 70, far in excess of the 48 that Truman's budget would fund. If approved, that would have cancelled $573m in contracts and to pay for existing programmes the proposed B-54 was stopped to help save the B-36. It was also instrumental in decisions over the fate of the YB-49 flying wing.

The air force proposed to spend $172m out of $270m in savings from cancelling other types, buying 39 additional B-36s and reconfiguring the B-36B for optimised developments. LeMay testified before Congressional hearings that the most effective way was to increase the inventory with two groups flying B-36s and retire two medium bomber (B-29/B-50) groups, with one strategic reconnaissance group equipped with RB-36s in lieu of RB-49s. Many of the decisions made between 1948 and 1950 were based

ABOVE: Displaying the round-tip propellers of the A and B variants, this B-36 at Albuquerque, New Mexico, shows off the sliding aft upper turret cover at an air show in August 1949. Frank Kleinwechter, scanned by Don Pettit via Dennis Jenkins

LEFT: With the introduction of the B-36 into SAC, a wide range of ancillary and support equipment was required to access all parts of this gigantic aircraft. Via Dennis Jenkins

Selected performance parameters for B-36A and B variants				
	B-36A Basic Mission	**B-36A Max Bombs**	**B-36B Basic Mission**	**B-36B Max Bombs**
T/O Weight	310,380lb (140,788kg)	311,000lb (141,069kg)	326,000lb (147,873kg)	317,500lb (144,018kg)
Load	10,000lb (4,536kg)	72,000lb (32,659kg)	10,000lb (4,536kg)	86,000lb (39,009kg)
T/O Distance	8,000ft (2,438m)	8,000ft (2,438m)	8,000ft (2,438m)	7,250ft (2,209m)
Climb rate	502ft/min (153m/min)	500ft/min (152m/min)	500ft/min (152m/min)	540ft/min (164m/min)
Max speed	339mph (546kph)	353mph (568kph)	389mph (625kph)	367mph (690kph)
Service ceiling	39,100ft (11,917m)	40,700ft (12,405m)	43,700ft (13,319m)	43,100ft (13,136m)
Combat radius	3,878miles (6,240km)	2,105miles (3,388km)	3,710miles (5,969km)	1,852miles (2,979km)
Landing Weight	158,080lb (71,705kg)	153,850lb (69,786kg)	163,321lb (74,082kg)	156,918lb (71,178kg)
Mission Time	35.6hrs	19.57hrs	38.45hrs	16.5hrs

Note: Values are expressed in statute miles and not nautical miles or knots. Figures may vary from official performance values which are in knots.

on the need for the US to maintain an effective air force in the wake of budget reductions, balanced against a still-worsening global threat to peace.

On June 25, 1950, the communist forces of North Korea poured south wreaking havoc and bringing South Korea close to collapse. Within days the United Nations pleaded with the United States to lead an allied force to expel the invaders and US Air Force staffers met to organise a major air war to support land and sea-based initiatives. Discussion surrounded the optimum use of strategic bombing operations with the B-29 and the B-50 at the forefront. There was also consideration of the B-36 being assigned to operate in anger, but the type was not yet ready for action and would be held back in case the war escalated into a conflict with China and perhaps with Russia too.

There was serious consideration of deploying the B-36 in a show of force and to a limited extent that was implemented (see page 80). While NATO armed forces rallied to support the UN's drive to remove North Korean troops from the south, planners at SAC mobilised revised attack plans which did include the use of the B-36 in diversionary attacks on targets in

China. An implied threat from Russia, suggesting that if that occurred, they would invade Western Europe, stayed the hand of proactive attack advocates such as LeMay and Power in much the way that Douglas MacArthur had been restrained by Truman over his proposal to attack China with atomic weapons.

The B-36 had been central to all these considerations and had already proved its worth, at a cost, but the type was in urgent need of a performance upgrade and there were no funds for a major development programme. With the B-52 underway, there was no additional money for different types to fill the intermediate role. The last of 62 B-36Bs was delivered in September 1950, by which date its successor variant was already entering service as the B-36D. It was a variant that many expected would be called on to drop bombs in anger.

B-36C

The performance of the B-36B had provided a baseline configuration considered suitable for further development. Confidence in the type, first from Convair and then the air force provided encouragement to seek ways of eliminating its weaknesses. These included a list of performance

increments headed by addressing the poor speed of the aircraft. Along with improved reliability and systems operability, the aircraft would benefit from different engines and attention switched to that issue.

Up for consideration was a turboprop variant, most favoured being the 5,500hp (4,101kW) Wright T-35 or the 10,000hp (7,457kW) Northrop T-37 Turbodyne, with either tractor or pusher engines buried in the wing. Several studies were conducted, but none were taken up. Yet the search for improved speed forced planners to think again and to power a new variant with the Variable Discharge Turbine (VDT). There had been considerable debate about the value of gas turbine engines and several turboprop derivatives in particular and the most accessible solution minimising design and engineering changes to the overall configuration of the aircraft was to select the VDT concept.

The NACA had conducted many studies of the VDT and were highly supportive of its potential. It had been sought by several manufacturers of experimental aircraft for its harvesting of wasted engine gases through the exhaust, but the compromises made in providing a reliable design for high-altitude work in very low temperatures was one problem difficult to solve. In principle the VDT solution was viable, but with the all-jet B-52 promising to outperform these reciprocating makeovers there was little point to its use in the B-36 programme.

Proposed VDT-powered aircraft had been given the designation B-36C and five airframes (44-92099 to 44-92103) had been cut out of the existing production order to compensate for cost inflation and to pay for the new project. With challenges to the overall budget, the US Air Force had no alternative but to cancel its order for the five C-series aircraft and to finish them to B-36D specification, with jet engines supplementing the reciprocating engines. A solution had been found to the slow speed of the aircraft but not in the way originally intended.

BELOW: Various engine arrangements were considered in an attempt to improve performance, including the VDT concept which proved too expensive and provide too little increase in speed. Convair

SUBSCRIBE TODAY!

Aeroplane is still providing the best aviation coverage around, with focus on iconic military aircraft from the 1930s to the 1960s.

Aviation News is renowned for providing the best coverage of every branch of aviation.

from our online shop...
/collections/subscriptions

Free 2nd class P&P on all UK & BFPO orders. Overseas charges apply.

Jet Power

The B-36 came of age with the addition of supplementary jet power and improved ways of operating with upgraded variants as the ten-engine behemoth entered the jet age.

Convair had searched for ways to give the B-36 better performance, greater altitude, faster speed over the target, and extended range. Much of that had been sought by the air force through line changes to the way the aircraft was operated. But that was tinkering at the margins. The only real increase would come from a revision in the accommodation for crew performance and provision of better propulsive power. When the VDT concept proved ineffective, the idea of using jet engines to augment the reciprocating engines was a natural progression. But there was no money for a radical solution, only appropriate use of existing technology and available engines were affordable in an age of tightened defence budgets.

Between 1945 and 1948 considerable improvement in jet engine efficiency made their use more desirable. Not yet as an exclusive replacement for the propeller-driven arrangement, but as a supplement during which the jets could be turned on and off as required, thus considerably reducing the disadvantage they had of high fuel consumption. The all-jet force of B-47s and B-52s was in active development and they would receive the benefit of a parallel investment in air-to-air refuelling tankers so that they could reach their targets. With them, total range was not as uncompromising a requirement as it was for the B-36, which had no such provision.

It was logical that with the enormous wing and the loads it was already built to carry, adding jet engines to the outer wing sections was a solution, one which would give the aircraft an extended life and broaden its ability to serve SAC with a stretched strategic war mandate. Accordingly, Convair conducted a new structural loads analysis and evaluated optional locations for jet engines. Engineers proposed a pair of General Electric J47 turbojets carried under each outer wing section. The number of modifications required for this adaptation were far less than those required for the cancelled VDT on the now defunct B-36C.

Convair promised the air force that it could have a flying conversion ready within four months of go-ahead, but authorisation to proceed was not received until January 4, 1949. Nevertheless, Convair continued to work on the detailed design of the augmentation and the first flight occurred as early as March 26, 1949, not as a contracted B-36D as frequently misidentified but of a converted B-36B (44-92057). This aircraft would be used for vibration and propeller tests with jet engines installed and would also conduct armament trials before it was accepted by the US Air Force in January 1951 and converted to a B-36D-40-CF after which

BELOW: *A B-36B (44-92036) converted to B-36D standard with paired J47 jet engine pods under each outer wing section. Note the open snap-doors for the bomb bays. Via Dennis Jenkins*

it joined the 92nd BW at Fairchild AFB, Spokane, Washington.

In several respects, the General Electric J47 was a product of desperation and was as new as the B-36 itself, the two sharing an unrelated but chronologically parallel development path without any consideration that they should blend together. But Convair sought a low-cost and readily available solution and the availability of the J47 and its selection by Boeing to power the B-47 provided benefit on both counts. Convair wanted to take the paired pods for two J47s as carried on the inboard wing sections of that medium bomber and marry them to outer wing sections on the B-36.

General Electric J47

General Electric had been selected to build the I-A engine to the original design of the Whittle W.1X and the Rover W.2B and as such it provided the engines for the Bell XP-59, the first US jet fighter, and the J33 for the P-80A Shooting Star. But it was unable to exploit that development further due to extreme demand for its turbo-superchargers and the J33 was licence-built by Allison. This did not completely stop GE from using that design as the basis for a further range of engine types, specifically the TG-180 which came straight from its T-31 turboprop engine and designated J35, the first axial-flow

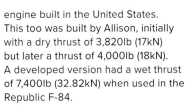

engine built in the United States. This too was built by Allison, initially with a dry thrust of 3,820lb (17kN) but later a thrust of 4,000lb (18kN). A developed version had a wet thrust of 7,400lb (32.82kN) when used in the Republic F-84.

Further work by GE on its TG-190 translated into the J47 when the air force took a strong interest and helped the company with test work and the encouragement of potential orders. The first J47 was test run on June 21, 1947, but problems plagued early evolution of the engine, weight being a particular challenge. Design changes solved most of those with materials playing a vital role in its operation and performance; engine development in the late 1940s was as much about different metals and alloys operating at unusually high temperatures as it was about compressors and turbines.

The J47 went into production in mid-1948 following a test flight in a

B-29 on April 20 and a test run in a P-86A (later F-86A) on May 18. On September 15, 1948, a standard F-86A with this engine stablished a new world speed record of 670.98mph (1,073kph). Suitably impressed, the US Air Force specified the J47 for the production F-86A and for the new, all-jet Boeing B-47, the latter carrying six engines, four in paired pods inboard and in single pods outboard on its highly swept wing.

The J47 had a twelve-stage axial-flow compressor with air flow introduced at 90lb/sec (40.8kg/sec) to a single-stage axial flow turbine with eight through-flow combustion chambers. Lubrication was provided by pressure feed to primary components with a return oil system to the bearings and the accessory gears. The electrical system consisted of a GE direct-drive starter-generator, two igniter-plugs and two ignition units. Overall, the J47 had a length of 144in (365.8cm), a diameter of 36.75in (93.3cm), a frontal

area of 7.4ft² (0.68m²) and a weight of approximately 2,500lb (1,135kg).

There was a delay in getting the desired engines in place for the first flight of what would be the B-36D configuration and the converted B-36Bs had four Allison J35-A-19 engines standing in for the J47s. The engines assigned to production aircraft was the J47-GE-19 turbojet with a rated thrust of 5,200lb (23.13kN) but some of the early engines were of the -11 configuration. As a special adaptation for the B-36, the engines had collapsible aerodynamic covers over the inlets to reduce drag when they were not in use. These allowed 5% of the air to flow through and keep the compressor turning so as to prevent them freezing up through icing.

Convair adopted the pods with minor changes, but they were almost identical to those designed and built for the inboard pair of engines on the

B-47 and initially the manufacturing of those continued for the B-36 with Boeing at Wichita since it was simpler to add production lots and then disperse delivery to the two programmes. For the B-47, pods for the single outer engines had outriggers attached to the underside of the casings, unnecessary for the B-36.

Modifications allowed for the use of standard aviation fuel rather than jet fuel used on the B-47 and the B-52, which also had J47 engines, so that feed could be configured from the existing integral tanks. This produced a slightly lower power output, but the advantage of the jet pods far outweighed the modest thrust reduction. Engine controls were situated on a panel above the pilots' heads and instruments were attached to two sub-panels below the main instrument panel, but the flight engineer was only provided with fire warning lights and nothing else.

From May 1951 pod production was switched to the Bell factory which was only 12 miles (19km) from Convair's Fort Worth facility. The XB-47 had made its first flight on December 17, 1947, but that was also made with the J35 as a stand-in for the J47 engines with which later production aircraft were fitted. With initial deliveries to the air force in 1951, the B-47 accompanied the definitive B-36D into service use but as a medium bomber.

Operations with the mixed-propulsion variants of the B-36 required ground technicians to receive specific instructions outlining the new danger from jet engine operations by intake cowlings painted bright red so as to give caution. This did not always work, and some incidents occurred when ground crew suffered burns while the jets were running on the ground together with the six reciprocating engines which deadened their sound. They also provided the pilots with visible indication of the proximity of the wing tips to ground obstacles and in the air provided a visual verification of the position of the collapsible covers.

The shift to an all-jet combat force for fighters and bombers propelled GE into the big business arena, growing from $35m at the end of World War Two to $350m by 1950 and after the start of the Korean War, output increased at an unprecedented rate. This financed a sustained development programme with the early A-series engine producing 4,850lb (21.57kN), the C-series pushing out 5,200lb (23.13kN) and 6,000lb (26.69kN) with water injection. The J-47-GE-25 which was developed for the B-47E produced 6,000lb (26.69kN) dry and 6,970lb (31kN) with water injection.

ABOVE: *Adding an additional thrust of 30,800lb (92.5kN), the four J47 engines transformed the B-36 programme with greatly enhanced performance.*
Vis Dennis Jenkins

LEFT: *Collapsible covers protected the J47 inlets and prevented icing at high altitude.*
Via Dennis Jenkins

although it was still to be seen on the B-36Bs modified into D types.

Convair received a contract for the B-36D on January 19, 1949, to cover 39 additional aircraft over and above the 95 already under the original contract (five having been deleted to compensate for added work on the jet pod conversion). Further contract extensions increased the added production lot to 75 aircraft by October that year, the first of several production extensions, but all were subsequently re-contracted into later variants.

Originally ordered as a B-36B, the first new-build production B-36D flew on July 11, 1949, and the air force received its first D-series (49-2653) on August 22, 1950. It went straight to the 11th Bomb Wing at Carswell but spent its life as a test aircraft at Eglin AFB while the 26 new-build D-series aircraft were all delivered by August 1951. The last carried the serial 49-2655 and was delivered later than its immediate predecessors as, by arrangement with

ABOVE: *A clear view of the clean wing with paired J47s for the D, H, and J variants of the B-36, the pods being part of the production run primarily committed to the B-47 medium bomber.* Via Dennis Jenkins

Production of J47 engines reached 950 per month shared with Studebaker and Packard, all of that a result of big budget increases stimulated by the Korean War. In all, some 36,500 engines of this type were produced at a record engine production rate unsurpassed to this day. With the Eisenhower administration (1953-1961) this was to tail off, but the J47 was in big demand. Nevertheless, the definitive J47-GE-33 produced a dry thrust of 7,650lb (34kN).

B-36D

As noted previously, the last 11 B-36Bs were completed to B-36D standard on the assembly line in the form of seven reconnaissance versions (see page 88) and four bomber configurations. Eventually, all B-36Bs were modified into the D-series. After the first four B-36Bs were converted (44-92026, 034, 053, and 054) the modification work shifted to the San Diego plant leaving the Fort Worth factory to produce all new, production-line B-36Ds.

The D-series type adopted the same 3,500hp (2,608kW) R-4360-41 reciprocating engine which had been fitted to the B-36B and although there would be a modest update to this engine, it would remain the same for subsequent variants of the bomber. The D-series also set the maximum gross weight which had increased to 357,000lb (161,935kg) and this would be retained across subsequent variants up to the B-36H. The B-36D also had the greatest quantity of magnesium applied to external surfaces, also replacing fabric-covered control surfaces. To this date, earlier variants had a retractable tail bumper, but this was eliminated from the D-series on,

RIGHT: *A plan view of the B-36D configuration with paired J47 turbojet engines.* Convair

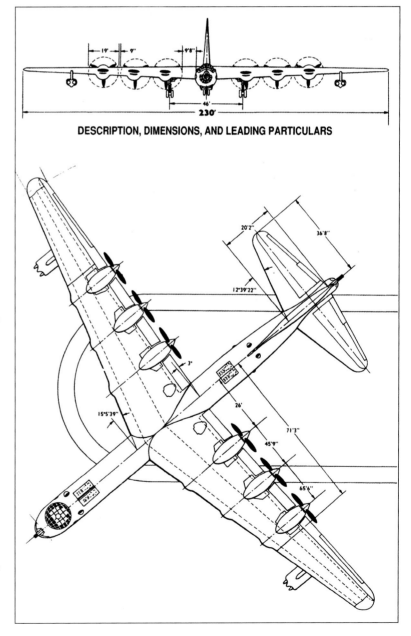

DESCRIPTION, DIMENSIONS, AND LEADING PARTICULARS

It was expected that the D-series would have the much improved K-3 bombing and navigation system but this proved problematic and initially the K-1 was installed offering very little advantage over the APQ-24, which had been standard in the B-36B. Special outdoor work docks were set up but the reassembly work was carried out on four aircraft simultaneously in Building 3, only the tail missing due to the height of the roof.

At San Diego since April 6, 1950, the first converted B-36B (44-92043) was returned to the air as a B-36D on December 5 following which, after two further flights, it was sent back to the air force on December 17. The final reworked aircraft ordered as a B-36B (92081) was re-delivered back to the air force on February 14, 1952. Significant requalification of the aircraft was required, and extensive checks were carried out on navigation equipment and especially on the defensive armament, with tests at Fort Worth consuming 200,000 rounds of 20mm cannon shells by the end of 1950!

From its first flight it was clear that the B-36D was a completely different aircraft to that which had been introduced into service a year before and with its uprated performance it was closer to initial expectation of this type when proposed in 1941. The supplementary jet engines produced an impressive increase in performance, some early boasts claiming a top speed of 439mph (706kph) at 32,120ft (9,790m) and a service ceiling of 45,020ft (13,722m). After much publicity surrounding these optimistic projections, and the end of the budget cycle for that year, the figures were

Convair, it had been used to evaluate various improvements to crew comfort.

B-36B conversion work began at San Diego with a complete overhaul, fitment of new control surfaces and snap-action bomb bay doors, which would become standard. These doors could open and close in two seconds and reduced drag. Two sets of doors were provided, one for the forward bays and the other for the rear pair and all B-36Ds were able to carry the Mk III atomic weapon in the forward bay. This location was the easiest to get to and would allow best access for arming the bomb in flight. Also replaced was the much improved AN/APG-32 tail radar over the APG-3 installed in the B-36B, although here too the converted B-36Bs initially had the older equipment.

In addition, all the outer wing panels were removed for strengthening, engines and associated accessories being sent to Kelly AFB for re-sealing of the integral fuel tanks and the fitting of new auxiliary tanks in the inner wing sections. Additionally, 13 US gal (49.2l lit) of oil for the jets was stored in 20 US gal (75.7 lit) tanks in the outer wing sections. Two 4,800 US gal (18,168 lit) supplementary fuel tanks were incorporated into the inboard wing sections, consisting of four bladder-like fuel cells manufactured from rubber impregnated with nylon fabric. These were not self-sealing or armoured,

but the exact capacity differed by up to 100 US gal (378 lit). It was still possible to house the single 3,000 US gal (11,355 lit) auxiliary tank in bomb bay No.3.

This work also provided opportunity to update the electronics and to fit new variants of existing equipment.

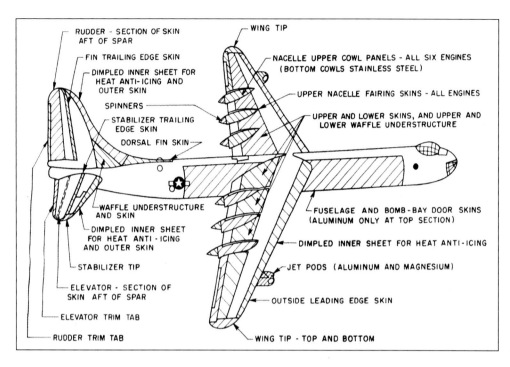

RUDDER - SECTION OF SKIN AFT OF SPAR

FIN TRAILING EDGE SKIN

DIMPLED INNER SHEET FOR HEAT ANTI-ICING AND OUTER SKIN

SPINNERS

STABILIZER TRAILING EDGE SKIN

DORSAL FIN SKIN

WAFFLE UNDERSTRUCTURE AND SKIN

DIMPLED INNER SHEET FOR HEAT ANTI-ICING AND OUTER SKIN

STABILIZER TIP

ELEVATOR - SECTION OF SKIN AFT OF SPAR

ELEVATOR TRIM TAB

RUDDER TRIM TAB

WING TIP

NACELLE UPPER COWL PANELS - ALL SIX ENGINES (BOTTOM COWLS STAINLESS STEEL)

UPPER NACELLE FAIRING SKINS - ALL ENGINES

UPPER AND LOWER SKINS, AND UPPER AND LOWER WAFFLE UNDERSTRUCTURE

FUSELAGE AND BOMB-BAY DOOR SKINS (ALUMINUM ONLY AT TOP SECTION)

DIMPLED INNER SHEET FOR HEAT ANTI-ICING

JET PODS (ALUMINUM AND MAGNESIUM)

OUTSIDE LEADING EDGE SKIN

WING TIP - TOP AND BOTTOM

ABOVE: *A map of materials and skins for the B-36 with a sectional layup guide for modellers.* Convair

revised downward to 406mph (653kph) at 36,200ft (11,034m) and a ceiling of 43,800ft (13,250m). Indisputably, the aircraft was more flexible and with jets on and all six reciprocating engines turning the take-off run was reduced by 2,000ft (610m) and the rate of climb almost doubled to 900ft/min (274m/min).

The aircraft was now able to exceed the operating ceiling of the jet fighters of the day, which were in any event unstable at that height due to the reduced atmospheric pressure on their low aspect-ratio wings. To a limited extent, it was the best of both worlds. At cruising altitude, the B-36D could shut down the jets and up to three piston engines, continuing to operate on just three of its ten engines. This conserved fuel and operational practice became

that the jets routinely operated only for take-off, for climb out, and for a dash across the target.

Quite quickly, SAC found the propaganda effect of the B-36D was enormous, drawing crowds whenever there was an open day at Fort Worth or an air show at which it appeared, and certainly during visits to overseas bases. On January 16, 1951, six B-36Ds arrived at RAF Lakenheath in the UK, having flown from Carswell, and staging through Limestone, Maine. Under the operational name 'United Kingdom', it was the type's first overseas goodwill visit. The visit was led by Colonel Thomas P Gerrity, the commander of the 11th BW at Carswell AFB and the six aircraft returned on January 20. The implication was not lost on the Russians.

The B-36D made a great impression on the British public and on the RAF too; to compare the enormous size of the B-36, a Gloster Meteor was positioned under one wing of the aircraft for Pathe News. It was also the first time anyone outside the United States had heard the extraordinary, and quite unique sound of the B-36, as can be testified to when this writer experienced the aircraft on that very visit in 1951, eyes lifted to the sky to see these strange looking aircraft passing overhead. As one reflective RAF veteran said, the B-36D was to the B-series what the Lancaster had been to the Manchester, receiving additional engines to realise the full potential of the airframe.

This visit to the UK combined a public relations exercise with a demonstration of improvements to crew comfort, acoustic panels being added in each pressure compartment to deaden the thunderous roar of the jet engines, 97 for the forward compartment and 59 for the aft compartment. They consisted of wool and fibreglass padding attached to specific areas and snap-fixed to the bulkheads. Due to the subtle changes appearing on the line, the original design was adjusted later so that each panel was sized to a specific location on a particular aircraft. More surprisingly, and uniquely to this aircraft, 30 sections of vinyl carpets were laid down and attached to the floor in the pressurised areas.

The crew complement was usually 14 but duties were shuffled slightly, consisting of pilot and co-pilot, two engineers, navigator, bombardier, two radio operators, a forward observer, and five gunners in the aft compartment. One of the two radio operators was also responsible for the electronic countermeasures (ECM) equipment. Along with the observer, one of the pilots also operated the forward upper gun turrets.

The crew improvement programme also included changes to the arrangement of a new galley in the aft compartment providing two cooking stoves in the form of electric burners together with pots and pans with lids, cooking utensils and cutlery including knives, forks, spoons, and ladles. Soup or drinks could be heated using a pair of plug-in hot cups and there was an electric oven for baking bread or preparing hot meals and general food supplies kept in a refrigerator. For eating meals, two folding tables were attached to opposing sides of the aft pressurised compartment with fold-down bunks doubling as chairs. In this way four men could eat in relative comfort. Meals prepared in the aft compartment could be taken along the pressurised tunnel to crew members in the forward compartment.

RIGHT: *The flight deck and pilot stations for the B-36D with modified yoke.* Via Dennis Jenkins

25-759   3-13-5
B-36F SHIP NO. 139 FLIGH
ENG. MAIN CONTROL PANE
CVAC FT WORTH TEXAS

on flight readiness after long-range missions. It was with this aircraft that the programme logged the longest flight achieved by the B-36 when it took off from Carswell AFB at 09.05 on January 14, 1951, and landed again at 12.35 on January 16, remaining airborne for 51 hours 30 minutes. The Convair crew had a demanding and full range of test objectives which had been followed on many other flights lasting in excess of 25 hours. This aircraft was eventually modified into a GRB-36D-1-CF for the FICON programme (see page 96) where it carried the RF-84F Thunderflash.

Extending the evaluation to operations and simulated attacks from foreign bases, on December 6, 1951, six B-36Ds from the 11th BW deployed to Sidi Slimane, French Morocco, in a flight covering the 5,000 miles (8,045km) in 20 hours, the new 'comfort packs' coming in for a real-world test and evaluation, much to the delight of the crew. Over the following years of active duty, the B-36 would visit this place many times, as well as the nearby airfield of Nouasseur AFB. But there was more to it than flexing the crews and checking out overseas deployments. It was a test of the aircraft's endurance and the ability of flight and ground crew to manage problems encountered because of the extreme range and flight time.

Throughout the early service years of the B-36D, a continuous flow of upgrades and improvements were incorporated on the production line and retrofitted to delivered aircraft. Modifications and improvements to the electrical systems reduced the risk of failure and fire, improved tank sealants were adopted, and the general awareness of failure indicators helped revise crew manuals on a frequent basis.

There was also an improvement in the toilet facilities in the aft compartment with a wash sink, a mirror, a commode, and a privacy curtain. Racks were added, attached to lugs between the bunks and luggage bins in the ceiling stowed crew kit where previously it had been kept on the floor. Where six bunks had been provided in the aft compartment for the resting crew, experience showed that most crew members located in the forward compartment slept in their seats so the B-36D had two foldaway bunks there.

A persistent problem on the B-36B was the Farrand Y-1 retractable periscope, changed to the non-retractable Y-3 on the D-series. This had a small periscope protruding from the starboard side of the under-fuselage, the port previously used for the Y-1 being covered with a fixed metal plate. The glazed nose was retained on the RB-36D variant as well as on B-36D aircraft fitted with the Norden sight, which came with its own windscreen wiper.

In several respects, the B-36D was a completely new aircraft and while general flying qualities remained remarkably similar to the B-series, there was a new performance capability which required extensive test and evaluation. The third B-36D (44-92090) was accepted by the US Air Force in January 1950 but immediately returned to Convair for a special fast-track programme. During the first 73 days it was in the air for 500 hours and subject to a full, seven-day inspection every 120 flying hours, duplicating an intensive operating schedule closely following air force requirements in wartime, to the extent that phantom bombing runs were conducted from 40,000ft (12,192m).

Endurance for the aircraft, its systems and the crew were fundamental to revising mission capabilities and writing up the flight operations handbooks. There was also a need to provide engineering calibration

92683

RIGHT: *The tight forward pressurised upper compartment on an RB-36H (50-1110) with navigator 1st Lieutenant James Shively (front left), photo-navigator Captain William Merrill (rear left), nose gunner and weather observer A1C Albert Brown (top centre) and radar observer Captain Franklin O'Donald.*
Via Dennis Jenkins

Additionally, new materials, some only appearing after the B-36D entered service, ensured improved safety features. Developed for Convair's CV-240 airliner, Proseal was used to fully close micro-size leak gaps in rivets and was applied to the 26,000 rivets in fuel tanks on the B-36, but the procedure was time-consuming, one man on a single working shift completing applications on 250 rivets. With added line experience and operating records, servicing and maintenance crews helped compile a log of improvements to forgings and castings, finding that the bulkheads and landing gear were particularly stressed.

Operations with aircraft of this size gave the B-36 special value to industry standards, for evaluating new techniques and materials on high-load types and for handling them on the apron and on the runway. Particular attention was paid to the landing gear struts and shock-absorbers, to the deployment and retraction gear and to their life cycle. Special attention was paid to the B-36D as the standard for later variants which would use this type as the benchmark for further improvements, modifications, and additions.

Although records show that only 26 B-36Ds were delivered, the majority of B-36Bs were brought up to D-series standard. The last B-36D was delivered in April 1951 and assigned to the 42nd BW. The flyaway cost of this variant was $4.1m, compared with $2.5m for the B-36B, of which 61% was in the 10 engines, less than 14% in electronics and 18% in

RIGHT: *Radio operator Staff Sergeant John McCarl at his station.*
Via Dennis Jenkins

defensive armament. The story of the 24 reconnaissance RB-36D production aircraft begins on page 88.

B-36F

There was no B-36E, that letter suffix being reserved for the reconnaissance variants but the next series, the B-36F, was contracted to Convair on April 13, 1949, but with a concurrent commitment to the B-36D. The only

visually noticeable difference with the B-36F was that it had the R-4360-53 engines with a rated 3,500hp (2,610kW), or 3,800hp (2,834kW) with water/ alcohol injection. This engine had been thoroughly evaluated on a B-36D (44-92054), introducing fuel injection with a redesigned ignition system, combinations which, along with 25 other changes, brought more than its share of problems during service life.

LEFT: *The display and control panel for the definitive Convair B-36J 52-2220 showing the capacious window screens.* John Rossino/ Lockheed Martin Code One

Nevertheless, the B-36F had a top speed increased to 417mph (671kph) and a service ceiling raised to 44,000ft (13,411m).

Other changes included a reconfiguration of the defensive equipment, initially by incorporating the new 2CFR87C-1 fire control system, which replaced the mechanical computing system of the B-36D, and which had a continuous, high-speed output. Along with this came greatly improved gyroscope measuring circuits, enhanced attack factors, and a much easier level of maintenance. From aircraft 50-1064 on, the enhanced C-2 version was fitted, which also featured the addition of Rhodes-Lewis gun chargers in an attempt to reduce dispersions during firing. Later aircraft were fitted with the AN/APG-32A tail radar with two antenna radomes and a larger radome fairing. It also had the K-3A bombing system.

In March 1951, a review board consisting of 18 men examined the B-36F and checked the numerous changes and detailed modifications which had been made. This included a full engine change to qualify procedures for field-operations with the R-4360-53. Several improvements to engine-change procedures had been developed with field technicians and Pratt & Whitney demonstrated improvements to handling to the review board which witnessed a full engine change in a record 42 minutes. The requirement here was to demonstrate a procedure whereby the original engine was removed and located on its handling dolly before the new engine was installed together with the propeller and air plug.

The first of 34 B-36Fs (49-2669) took to the skies on November 18, 1950, but six (49-2703, 04, 05, 49-2670, 71, and 72) were set aside for a series of rapid service tests focused on the new engine, which was suspected of causing trouble. Convair conducted inspections

every 100 flying hours and the tests were completed on July 11, 1951, before the first US Air Force B-36F (49-2671) was handed over to the 7th BW/9th BS on August 18. It turned out that the new engines quickly settled in to a reliable service life with maintenance tasks reduced, due largely to the adoption of fuel injection, which had initially given unsubstantiated cause for concern.

While considered a great improvement on the B and D variants, the B-36F suffered a disproportionately high number of accidents, the first of which was on March 6, 1952, when 50-1077 suffered a failed main landing gear while on the ramp at Carswell AFB and burned. This prompted a universal inspection of all aircraft in the inventory and a number of modifications were authorised, conducted at facilities at San Diego, Fort Worth and San Antonio. On

August 5, 1952, fuel vapours through the No.3 tank vent on 49-2679 were ignited by exhaust from a power unit nearby, completely destroying the aircraft which had been on the inventory of the 7th BW/436th BS.

B-36H/J

It is often said there was no B-36G, except there was for a very brief period when two B-36Bs (49-2676 and 49-2684) were converted into an all-jet configuration with wings swept to 38° and set on an extended fuselage with a length of 171.2ft (52.18m). Powered by eight J57 engines in four underwing pods similar to those on the B-52, US Air Force authorisation was granted on March 16, 1951, and the B-36G made its first flight on April 18, 1952, from Fort Worth, but was quickly re-designated as the YB-60A. The XB-52 made its first flight three days later. The second aircraft never flew, and the programme was cancelled on January 20, 1953, after the XB-52 began flight tests and proved that the YB-60A was outclassed.

Several changes denoted the next variant, the B-36H, which was similar in essential aspects to the B-36F but with the K-series ECM relocated to the forward pressurised compartment for ease of maintenance and an additional station for the second flight engineer plus a redesigned instrument panel for the two pilots. Improvements were also made to the defensive armament by fitting dynamic gun mountings to prevent fire dispersion by mounting it on a spring cushion so that it could translate back and forth on tracks to transmit shock through springs rather than directly to the turret.

BELOW: *A map of fuel tank locations and bulk capacities for the B-36H and J series.* Convair

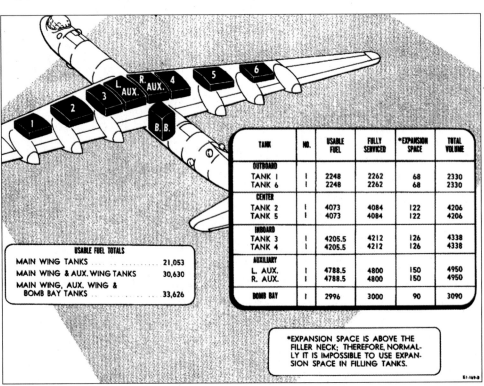

USABLE FUEL TOTALS

MAIN WING TANKS	21,053
MAIN WING & AUX. WING TANKS	30,630
MAIN WING, AUX, WING & BOMB BAY TANKS	33,626

TANK	NO.	USABLE FUEL	FULLY SERVICED	*EXPANSION SPACE	TOTAL VOLUME
OUTBOARD					
TANK 1	1	2248	2262	68	2330
TANK 6	1	2248	2262	68	2330
CENTER					
TANK 2	1	4073	4084	122	4206
TANK 5	1	4073	4084	122	4206
INBOARD					
TANK 3	1	4205.5	4212	126	4338
TANK 4	1	4205.5	4212	126	4338
AUXILIARY					
L. AUX.	1	4788.5	4800	150	4950
R. AUX.	1	4788.5	4800	150	4950
BOMB BAY	1	2996	3000	90	3090

*EXPANSION SPACE IS ABOVE THE FILLER NECK; THEREFORE, NORMALLY IT IS IMPOSSIBLE TO USE EXPANSION SPACE IN FILLING TANKS.

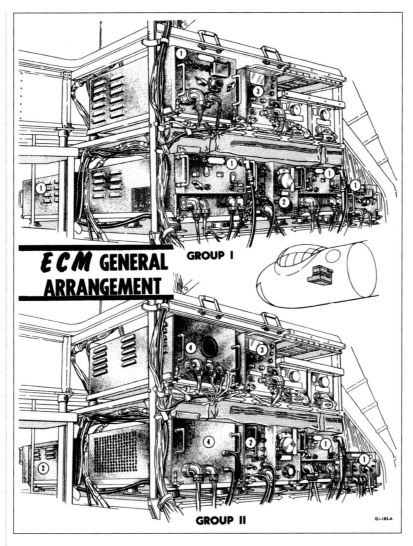

ECM GENERAL ARRANGEMENT

GROUP I

GROUP II

GI-183-A

adding extra space on the flight deck by moving the flight engineer's panel aft by 12in (30.5cm), and shortening the pilot's pedestal by six inches (15.2cm), which improved the path for emergency escape if the co-pilot and the assistant flight engineer had to take to their parachutes.

Aircraft subsequent to 51-5742 were equipped with a new AN/APG-41, gun-laying tail radar with twin tail radomes. This was two APG-32s coupled with one tracking immediate threats and the second for scanning the sky to detect approaching threats, the left-hand radar scanning aft from 60° right to 80° left while the right-hand unit, also facing aft, could scan 80° to the right and 60° to the left.

New for the B-36H were square-tipped propeller blades fitted as standard which improved both vibration levels and provided greater efficiency at higher altitude. Overall, flying performance of the B-36 had been compromised by the original propeller design consisting of three 19ft (5.79m) blades. The new four-bladed, 16ft (4.8m) propeller was a significant improvement and this variant also carried an improved ECM package and two A-6 or A-7 dispensers with 1,400lb (635kg) of chaff, a system retrofitted to late B-36Fs.

The initial announcement of the B-36H was made on November 5, 1950 and the flight of the first of 83 (50-1083) took place on April 5, 1952. Eight months later the type was entering service with SAC, later than planned due to a pause while tests on pressure bulkheads was made after one failed on a RB-36F at 33,000ft (10,058m) causing a temporary ban on all types exceeding 25,000ft (7,620m).

Alterations were also made to the lighting across the several crew stations and a complete mock-up for a new cockpit layout was inspected in August 1950, improvements which would follow with the J-series variant. At the inspection, revisions were requested and these included changing the pilot's gyro horizon which was too small and prone to being unreliable,

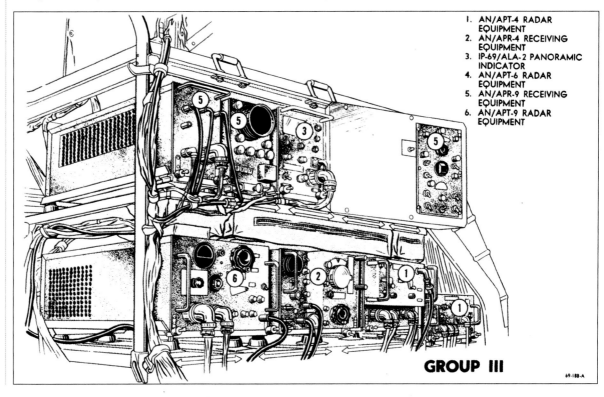

1. AN/APT-4 RADAR EQUIPMENT
2. AN/APR-4 RECEIVING EQUIPMENT
3. IP-69/ALA-2 PANORAMIC INDICATOR
4. AN/APT-6 RADAR EQUIPMENT
5. AN/APR-9 RECEIVING EQUIPMENT
6. AN/APT-9 RADAR EQUIPMENT

GROUP III

69-183-A

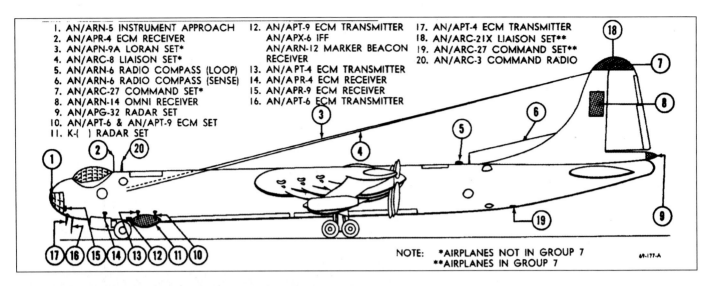

1. AN/ARN-5 INSTRUMENT APPROACH
2. AN/APR-4 ECM RECEIVER
3. AN/APN-9A LORAN SET*
4. AN/ARC-8 LIAISON SET*
5. AN/ARN-6 RADIO COMPASS (LOOP)
6. AN/ARN-6 RADIO COMPASS (SENSE)
7. AN/ARC-27 COMMAND SET*
8. AN/ARN-14 OMNI RECEIVER
9. AN/APG-32 RADAR SET
10. AN/APT-6 & AN/APT-9 ECM SET
11. K-( ) RADAR SET

12. AN/APT-9 ECM TRANSMITTER
    AN/APX-6 IFF
    AN/ARN-12 MARKER BEACON
    RECEIVER
13. AN/APT-4 ECM TRANSMITTER
14. AN/APR-4 ECM RECEIVER
15. AN/APR-9 ECM RECEIVER
16. AN/APT-6 ECM TRANSMITTER

17. AN/APT-4 ECM TRANSMITTER
18. AN/ARC-21X LIAISON SET**
19. AN/ARC-27 COMMAND SET**
20. AN/ARC-3 COMMAND RADIO

NOTE: *AIRPLANES NOT IN GROUP 7
**AIRPLANES IN GROUP 7

69-177-A

An unfortunate set of incidents and a tragedy occurred in succession during a visit by 18 B-36Hs from the 7th BW/492nd BS at Carswell to RAF Fairford in the UK during February 1953, a simulated mission with the code name Styleshow. One of the aircraft developed technical trouble on the flight east and returned home, the other 17 heading on across the Atlantic after staging through Goose Bay, Newfoundland. Sixteen aircraft landed safely but one (51-5719) had to hold due to bad weather and

missed two GCA approaches, largely due to inexperienced staff at the base. The aircraft had to be abandoned in flight, but the crew parachuted to safety.

The exercise proceeded with training missions out of RAF Fairford. Fourteen aircraft returned home on February 13 but two remained in the UK for specialised training. Of those returning to the US, a further misdirection from the Goose Bay GCA caused 51-5729 to fly into a hill, killing two of the 17 crew on board. The 13 remaining aircraft

arrived back at Carswell on February 21 followed by the two other aircraft from the UK two days later.

Unlikely as it seems today, under a mandate to equip all SAC aircraft for mid-air refuelling, Convair was asked to adapt a B-36H (51-5706) as a potential top-up station for its jet bomber force, adding a greater potential to its expanding inventory of KC-97 and KB-29 tankers. There had never been serious consideration of the B-36 being developed into a tanker but with the universal edict that all bombers in the inventory should have this capability, on January 15, 1952, authorisation was passed for such a conversion, known as the B-36 XIV, after the Mk XIV refuelling reel for a probe-and-drogue system.

Dubbed TanBo (tanker-bomber), the adapted aircraft carried a large hose reel in bomb bay No.4 with bladder tanks in the other three bays storing almost 16,000 US gal (60,560 lit) of jet fuel which the system could transfer to a connected fighter at a rate of 600 US gal/min (2,279 lit/min). A Republic F-84 was used for trials that began in March 1953, but the British-built system was not completely compatible, and tests ended on May 27. The aircraft was passed over to another programme for development of a stand-off capability with the Bell GAM-63 RASCAL (Radar

ABOVE: *Antenna and radio/radar equipment locations are displayed on the side-profile of a B-36H configuration.* Convair

LEFT: *The YB-60 was a fruitless attempt to challenge the B-52 and to present a potential replacement had that programme failed.* Convair

	Selected performance parameters for B-36D and B-36J			
	B-36D Basic Mission	**B-36D Max Bombs**	**B-36J Basic Mission**	**B-36J Max Bombs**
T/O Weight	370,000lb (167,832kg)	370,000lb (167,832kg)	410,000lb (185,976kg)	410,000lb (185,976kg)
Load	10,000lb (4,536kg)	72,000lb (32,659kg)	10,000lb (4,536kg)	72,000lb (32,659kg)
T/O Distance	5,685ft (1,732m)	5,685ft (1,732m)	6,820ft (2,078m)	6,820ft (2,078m)
Climb rate	970ft/min (295.6m/min)	970ft/min (295.6m/min)	780ft/min (237m/min)	780ft/min (237m/min)
Max speed	417mph (670kph)	425mph (683kph)	417mph (670kph)	425mph (683kph)
Service ceiling	35,000ft (10,668m)	38,300ft (11,673m)	43,600ft (13,289m)	46,500ft (14,173m)
Combat radius	3,751miles (6,035km)	2,169miles (3,490km)	3,987miles (6,415km)	2,497miles (4,017km)
Landing Weight	182,900lb (82,963kg)	180,490lb (81,870kg)	190,750lb (86,525kg)	187,590lb (85,090kg)
Mission Time	33.7hrs	18.3hrs	34.6hrs	20.9hrs

Note: Maximum speed and service ceiling varied widely with load and can differ when quoted in operating manuals, frequently the source of 'claimed' performance figures.

ABOVE: *The last B-36J leaves the assembly line, end of an era in which the US Air Force operated its final piston-powered bomber. Via Dennis Jenkins*

RIGHT: *With eight J57 turbojet engines, the YB-60 took to the air for the first time on April 18, 1952. USAF*

BELOW: *With a standard B-36 in the background, the YB-60A resembles its origins only in the forward fuselage which retains the original nose configuration. Convair*

Scanning Link), which had been authorised on July 7, 1952 and which would involve H-series aircraft.

Development of a long-range standoff missile began in May 1947 when Bell began work on RASCAL, eventually assigned for use with B-36 and B-47 aircraft. Powered by a XLR67 rocket motor, it was capable of Mach 3 after release from the bomb bay with a range of 100 miles (160km) carrying a nuclear warhead to its target. With a total length of 32ft (9.75m) with fore and aft trapezoidal aero-surfaces for a maximum span of 16.7ft (5.1m) and a loaded weight of 18,200lb (8,255kg) it was never operationally assigned to the B-36.

One aircraft designated YDB-36H (50-5710) was assigned to tests, with 12 H-series to be modified for carrying one RASCAL, semi-submerged in bomb bays three and four. The first flight took place in September 1952 from a modified B-50D with the first air-drop from the YDB-36H on August 25, 1953, but the programme was shifted to the B-47 and the B-36 had no further part to play. The small contribution to this

programme by the B-36 marked it as the first air-to-surface standoff weapon developed to this level by the US Air Force, a precedent for the Skybolt and cruise missiles of a later generation. RASCAL was cancelled in 1958.

The final production variant carried two extra fuel tanks in each outer wing section and the first of 33 B-36Js (52-2210) flew in July 1953 and was accepted by the air force the following

month. It also had a significant increase in maximum weight and was distinguishable for an elongated radome for the two antennas of the APG-41A gun-laying radar in the tail, equipment which was also fitted to some B-36H models. Watched by 11,000 people, the last B-36J (52-2827), and the last of 385 B-36s, rolled out on August 10, 1954, and was delivered to SAC four days later.

Warloads

Capable of carrying every bomb in the USAF arsenal, a single B-36 could deliver as much explosive power as that produced by every bomb dropped in anger during two world wars.

At its inception, the B-36 was expected to carry large bombloads which at the time meant conventional explosives of different types and for specialised purposes. During its design and development prior to August 1944, nobody directly associated with the programme at Convair knew about the atomic bomb or that the B-36 would be called upon to carry it. Until he replaced Franklin D Roosevelt as US President in April 1945, even Harry Truman knew nothing of the atom bomb. The US Army Air Force had little understanding of the impact it would have on future planning and not until the end of that year did the first plans for its deployment and integration into war-fighting plans begin to take shape, a story starting on page 34.

When the war with Japan ended in September 1945, the USAAF had begun to assign specific bomb types to various mission objectives for the Peacemaker. Significant among which

was the T-series adapted from the British Tallboy and Grand Slam bombs, which Convair was directed to apply to B-36 capabilities on August 14. By the time the atomic bombs were dropped on Hiroshima and Nagasaki, progress had been made with development of the 12,662lb (5,743kg) T-10, the 25,037lb (11,357kg) T-14 and the 44,000lb (19,958kg) T-12, which were to have been used against Japanese targets had the war continued.

Convair had already made progress with provision on the B-36 for carrying 67 different types of munition, including high explosive bombs, incendiary bombs, chemical bombs, and a wide range of different mines. The basic design of the four bomb bays allowed simultaneous carriage of 15 different munitions on 36 racks and there was discussion about a very special conventional bomb with a weight of 75,000lb (34,020kg). This was never fully developed but it emphasised the growth in weight-lifting requirements.

Of passing note, even the B-52 was unable to carry the Tallboy due to length limitations of its bay.

Convair had a head-start on development of the B-36's bomb bays and support equipment, adapting the configuration from a design previously employed on the B-24. The doors for the B-36A and B series were electrically-controlled and cable-operated to slide on tracks up the side of the fuselage. The doors covering bays one and four were single-piece units sliding up the left side while the doors for bays two and three were split at the centreline and would slide up opposing sides of the fuselage because the location of the wing prevented a single-piece enclosure. A problem with severe drag when the doors were open was solved by a new snap-action design.

The B-36D and subsequent variants had two door-sets, each set 32.37ft (9.86m) long and hydraulically operated with a fast, double-folding action which opened and closed them in two seconds. These snap-action doors had hydraulically actuated rams with each door 16.1ft (4.9m) long covering bomb bays one and two and three and four, respectively. The doors tended to stick, particularly in cold weather and at extreme altitude.

Made possible by significant structural changes, the enormous bomb-carrying capacity was set at a theoretical 86,000lb (39,001kg) in the B-36B, a 19% increase over the B-36A in a specification set before the US entered the war with

weapon. Developed by Bell, again from the design of the British Tallboy bomb, the Tarzon was 25ft (7.62m) in length and 54in (137.2cm) in diameter but it was developed too late to see service in World War Two. It was evaluated with the B-29 during the Korean War with 30 bombs dropped between December 1950 and August 1951 displaying a success rate of around 25% against bridges and hard targets.

Although the B-36 was designed to carry every available bomb in the US inventory, different types of munition in combinations which spanned 10,000lb (4,536kg) to 86,000lb (39,001kg), bombing-up required different techniques depending upon the size of the bomb. Ordnance up to 4,000lb (1,814kg) used standard external C6 or C10 bomb hoists attached to the upper spine and on top of the fuselage. Holes in the upper fuselage allowed the hoists to be suspended from the top and lowered down inside the fuselage to the hard stand below where the bombs were attached and winched up to their respective positions, all four bays were capable of being loaded simultaneously. Bigger conventional, atomic, and thermonuclear bombs would be loaded by hydraulic ramps.

Under normal application, while different types of bomb could be carried in individual bays, each bay was restricted to one type of bomb. At each end of the bay-spread, numbers one and four could contain up to 38 500lb (227kg) bombs, 19 1,000lb (453kg), eight 2,000lb (907kg), or four 4,000lb (1,814kg) bombs. In addition, bays two and three had a different configuration because they were not as vertically spacious due to the wing carry-through structure, although each could support 28 500lb (227kg), 16 1,000lb (453kg), six 2,000lb (907kg) or three 4,000lb (1,814kg) bombs.

In a modified configuration, bays one and two or three and four could be adapted to accommodate two 12,000lb (5,443kg) bombs, one 22,000lb (9,979kg) or one 43,000lb (19,505kg) bomb. Very little work was required to open up the division between the two forward and two aft bomb bays, requiring only the removal of dividing bulkheads. There were 15 types of bomb carriage for ordnance weighing up to 4,000lb (1,814kg), the racks being attached either side of the bay with larger bombs slung on suspension slings and shackles.

The capacity of the B-36 was considerably greater than that of the

RIGHT: *Two T-12 Tallboy bombs being loaded into the B-36 No.2 bay on January 29, 1949.* Via Dennis Jenkins

Germany, Italy, and Japan. This increase allowed the type to carry two 43,000lb (19,505kg) bombs in a system that retained the same configuration of bay doors as that on the A-series, a capacity which would make the B-36 the most significant bomb truck in the inventory.

Despite the universality of configurations there were always special munitions for specific types of target. Eighteen B-36Bs were fitted with the required guidance equipment for two 13,000lb (5,897kg) VB-13 Tarzon guided bombs. These were controlled by a radio link to the operator viewing a TV screen showing a picture transmitted from an optical device in the nose of the

RIGHT: *The four bomb bays separated into two sets by the wing carry-through structure with the access tunnel between pressurised compartments.* Convair

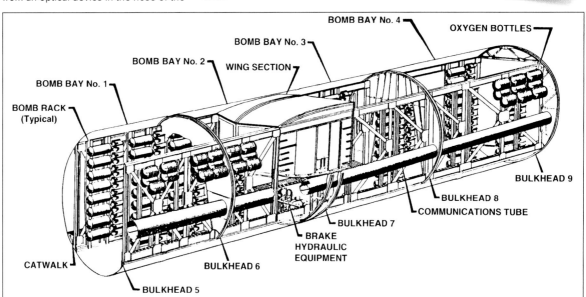

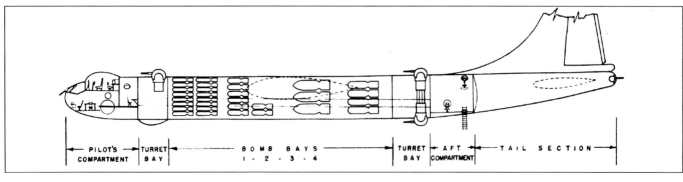

PILOT'S COMPARTMENT | TURRET BAY | BOMB BAYS 1 · 2 · 3 · 4 | TURRET BAY | AFT COMPARTMENT | TAIL SECTION

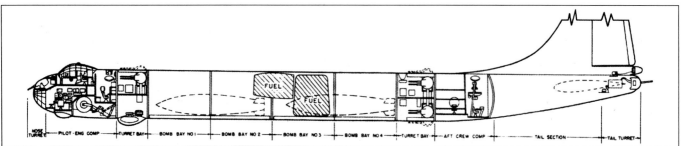

NOSE TURRET | PILOT · ENG COMP | TURRET BAY | BOMB BAY NO 1 | BOMB BAY NO 2 | BOMB BAY NO 3 | BOMB BAY NO 4 | TURRET BAY | AFT CREW COMP | TAIL SECTION | TAIL TURRET

early B-52 variants, even in its 'Big Belly' modification during the Vietnam conflict, where a theoretical capacity of 75,000lb (34,020kg) was offered. In addition, a 3,000 US gal (11,355 lit) removable fuel tank could be carried in bay No.3, although this was for special flights. Some aircraft were capable of carrying a similar tank in bay two but there has been unsubstantiated reference to bays one and four carrying tanks of similar capacity. Nothing in official documents verifies this, but a considerable amount of adaptation to unit requirements was common.

When carried, the auxiliary fuel tank consisted of a metal frame within which was suspended a fuel-proof rubberised canvas bag manufactured by Firestone Tire and Rubber Company. On later versions of the tank produced by Goodyear at their Akron, Ohio, facility, a Pliocell nylon bladder was supported by a metal encapsulating shell. Either tank design could be jettisoned during flight, after all the connections and fuel lines had been dismantled by hand. Uniquely for this aircraft, the bays could also carry support equipment including ground power start-up carts, and up to 14,000lb (6,350kg) of ancillary equipment, two carts stowed in Bay Nos.1 and four and a single cart in the other two. And of course, as noted earlier, additional piston engines could be air-lifted in panniers attached to the forward fuselage.

Atomic Air Force

When the B-36 became operational in 1948, only six B-29 crews with the 509th BW were proficient at dropping atomic weapons although the, albeit slow, uptake of atomic bomb production and testing in the US Air Force allowed the B-36 time to iron out bugs and prepare the aircraft for its primary role. It was imperative that any future US bomber be capable of carrying atom bombs, which the XB-35/YB-49 types could not, due to the limited size of their bomb bays. With a diameter of five feet (1.5m) and a length of 10ft (3m), the Mk III bomb was too large for these flying wing designs and even the B-29 and the B-50 were incapable of carrying bombs with a length greater than 12ft (3.6m).

Airframe manufacturers were denied access to proposed bomb configurations and the definitive design frequently bore little resemblance to the original specification regarding casings and mountings. Even the air force was uncertain as to what it was going to get in terms of bomb shape, centre of gravity, mounting lugs and

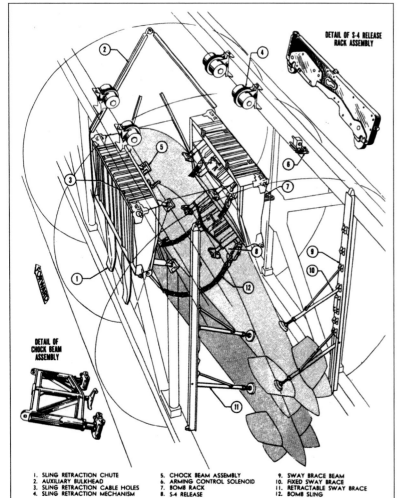

DETAIL OF S-4 RELEASE RACK ASSEMBLY

DETAIL OF CHOCK BEAM ASSEMBLY

1. SLING RETRACTION CHUTE
2. AUXILIARY BULKHEAD
3. SLING RETRACTION CABLE HOLES
4. SLING RETRACTION MECHANISM
5. CHOCK BEAM ASSEMBLY
6. ARMING CONTROL SOLENOID
7. BOMB RACK
8. S-4 RELEASE
9. SWAY BRACE BEAM
10. FIXED SWAY BRACE
11. RETRACTABLE SWAY BRACE
12. BOMB SLING

TOP: *The standard bay configuration for the four bays also showing the location of the defensive gun turrets. Convair*

ABOVE: *Optional upload of the additional fuel tank and the T-series, Tallboy bombs. Convair*

LEFT: *The relative stowage locations for two T-14 bombs in bays one and two. USAF*

RIGHT: *A Universal Bomb System installed in a B-36H with adaptation for carrying atomic and nuclear weapons.* National Archives College Park Collection via Dennis Jenkins

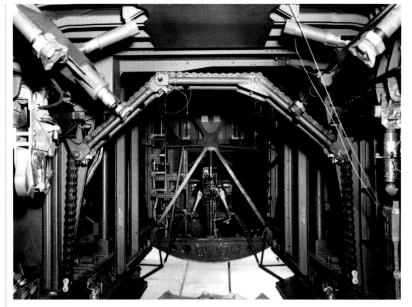

ballistic dynamics after release – crucial in case the bomb adversely reacted to the airstream after it had been released and 'floated' back up into the bay! Only gradually could the air force convince the Atomic Energy Commission that that they were working for the same country and against a common enemy, after which restrictions were lifted.

In this early period of building an atomic air force, it was forbidden to look up into the open bomb bay of a B-36 for fear that disclosure could lead to calculation of the size of bomb carried, thence to its destructive yield and so pose a security threat to the United States! This practice was retained well into the 1960s, as this writer can testify. The undying belief that the atom bombs dropped on Hiroshima

and Nagasaki had ended a global war bestowed almost god-like powers on the capacity of nuclear weapons not only to start wars but stop them. Hence the reverence with which they were treated – at least initially.

Introduced in 1952, the 8,800lb (3,855kg) Mk 6 was the first production A-bomb with over 1,000 manufactured by 1955, its introduction being compromised by the secretive nature of its size and weight until shortly before the USAF received it. But these problems were alleviated by the time the Mk 17 was introduced in 1954, a massive thermonuclear bomb 24.6ft (7.5m) in length and 5.08ft (1.55m) in diameter weighing 42,000lb (19,051kg) and with a weaponised yield of up to 15MT. The B-36 was the only aircraft that could carry this

fusion weapon, together with the indistinguishable Mk. 24.

Work to convert both the B-36 and the B-29 to carry the Mk III bomb came under the code name 'Saddle Tree'. This required the fitting of suspension equipment and T-boxes and the first 18 B-36Bs were so modified by June 1948, with the last 54 B-series equipped off the production line to carry it in bay one. Modifications to carry the Mk IV, Mk V, and Mk 6 began in December 1950 along with the Universal Bomb Suspension (UBS) system, capable of handling any weapon up to five feet (1.5m) in diameter and 10.7ft (3.26m) in length. These weapons had to be armed manually from the nose point on the bomb and the No.1 bay was the optimum place for crew access.

Only the B-36 could carry the Mk 17/24 type, two capable of being accommodated in the paired Nos.1/2 and 3/4 bomb bays. Tested during Operation Castle at Bikini atoll in 1954, they were differentiated by the different primaries they employed, each however utilising lithium hydride rather than the rare lithium-6 deuteride. They were equipped with a retarding parachute which would still have left the B-36 uncomfortably close to the blast effect. With the widest selection of conventional, nuclear (fission), and thermonuclear (fusion) weapons carried by any aircraft in the US inventory, the B-36 was the US Air Force's first 'Big Stick', bearing the distinction of being the only intercontinental bomber in history capable of delivering nuclear Armageddon to any hostile state anywhere on Earth without aerial refuelling.

RIGHT: *The auxiliary fuel tank consisted of a rigid shell containing a flexible bladder, the unit raised up into the bay using the overhead lift system.* Convair

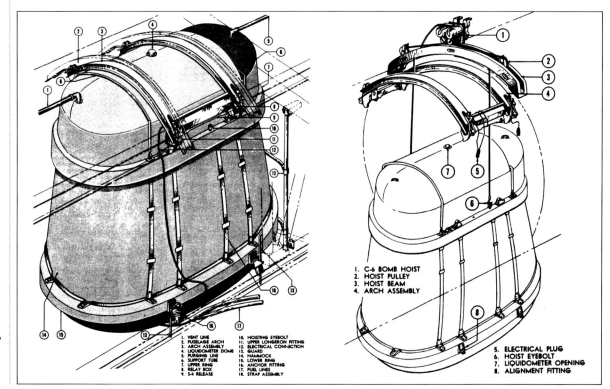

1. VENT LINE
2. FUSELAGE ARCH
3. ARCH ASSEMBLY
4. LIQUIDOMETER DOME
5. PURGING LINE
6. SUPPORT TUBE
7. UPPER RING
8. RELAY BOX
9. S-4 RELEASE
10. HOISTING EYEBOLT
11. UPPER LONGERON FITTING
12. ELECTRICAL CONNECTION
13. GUARD
14. HAMMOCK
15. LOWER RING
16. ANCHOR FITTING
17. FUEL LINES
18. STRAP ASSEMBLY

1. C-6 BOMB HOIST
2. HOIST PULLEY
3. HOIST BEAM
4. ARCH ASSEMBLY

5. ELECTRICAL PLUG
6. HOIST EYEBOLT
7. LIQUIDOMETER OPENING
8. ALIGNMENT FITTING

It turned out that the defensive armament for B-36 was the heaviest and most comprehensive suite of guns and associated equipment ever carried by any US combat aircraft. The configuration changed over time, and the positions of guns and turrets varied in two principal phases. Determination as to the type and calibre of gun was decided through a series of extensive analyses, some of which were noted earlier in this publication, producing information about where and from what direction the aircraft was exposed to attack.

Some of that information came from experience during World War Two, from studies of how B-17 armament changed over time, and from tactics known to have been used by Russian fighters. The defensive weapons configuration also had to be sufficiently flexible to introduce a continually evolving range of remotely controlled gun positions with electronic acquisition and tracking from radar and target sensors. There was considerable debate within the aircraft armament fraternity regarding the balance between manually-controlled guns and those, either singly or in pairs, which could be operated by autonomous systems.

The basic defensive concept had several optional gun types, the 0.60 calibre being set against the 0.50 calibre with the 20mm cannon being seen as a compromise between those, although it had lower ballistic properties and less destructive effect. Initially the B-36 had defensive positions at five locations, but the arrangement changed as to where those were situated. All the retractable turrets were capable of being withdrawn below the mould line and the openings covered with sliding panels to create a drag-free surface.

In production aircraft there were six paired turrets located in the forward and aft positions on top of the fuselage, from just behind the glazed pressure compartment and the vertical tail, and a paired turret on the aft fuselage, underside directly below the one on top. In addition, there were fixed tail

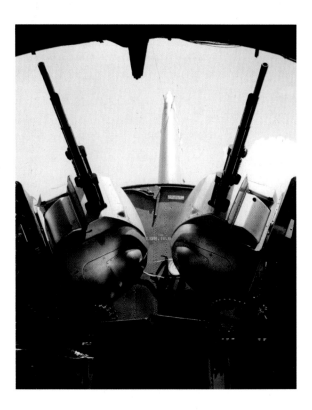

Turrets and Guns

Fighters and attack aircraft predating on the B-36 were a constant threat for mission planners, pitching against them the most extensive defensive armament of any aircraft in history.

and nose positions for eight defensive stations with their own fields of fire. The original concept had a pair of turrets on the forward fuselage underside as well, but that was removed to make way for the bomb/navigation radome and replaced by the nose guns.

The electrically-controlled turrets were operated from a sighting position located separately from the turret itself with three such positions located on each side of the fuselage, one forward and two aft. The nose section supported a sight in the glazed bombardier's position and the tail turret was controlled by a radar operator's position in the aft compartment. Yoke sights were set up in the four upper blisters for controlling those fore and aft turrets and they could

be rotated between +90° to -45° in elevation with reference to the horizon and from 110° forward to 110° aft of the transverse axis (wing-tip to wing-tip). The lower turret employed pedestal sights which could cover elevation angles from -45° to +90° in elevation and rotated in azimuth from +105° forward to -105° aft. In both yoke and pedestal sights the gunners traversed the entire sight to follow a target.

Operation of the sight required some training and considerable skill to provide accurate and useable information to the computer dedicated to that sight. Each sight had a small glass plate which the gunner powered up to present a centre dot for aiming and a series of concentric dots. The gunner would set the wing

span of the incoming attacker by means of a knob to align it with the dots which would set the range. By precisely tracking the motion of the attacker the computer would derive azimuth and elevation values and compute the relative speed by calculating the angular velocity from the motion scan.

The nose turret was controlled from a hemispheric sight to the starboard side of the nose containing a double prism periscope for a full hemispheric view by the gunner who, from a fixed position, could see 90° up, down, left, or right through a fixed eyepiece. Control of the guns was maintained by handles either side of the sight. It worked much like the yoke and the pedestal sights, with the gunner using a single eyepiece for one eye but an optional left or right eye according to the visual preferences of the operator. The radar-controlled tail turret was operated by a single gunner seated in the rear compartment and facing aft but in reconnaissance variants this position was sometimes shifted to a sideways-facing orientation.

Two guns were optional for each turret, the M24A1 or the M24E2, either with a selectable rate of fire between 550 and 820 rounds per minute on the earlier production aircraft or a fixed 700 rounds per minute for later aircraft. Usually left open during taxiing, because they served as emergency ground exits, the retractable

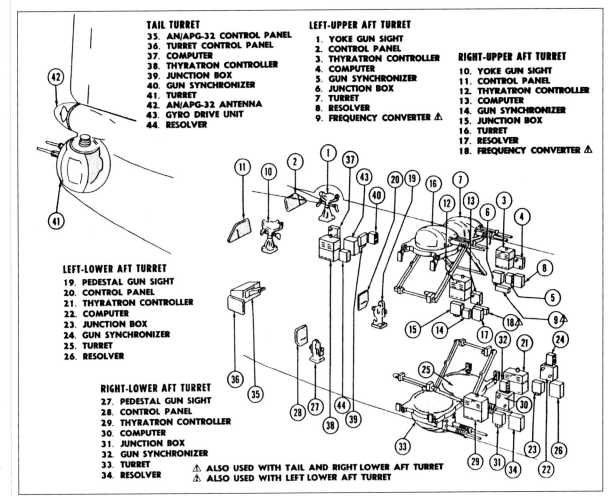

TAIL TURRET
35. AN/APG-32 CONTROL PANEL
36. TURRET CONTROL PANEL
37. COMPUTER
38. THYRATRON CONTROLLER
39. JUNCTION BOX
40. GUN SYNCHRONIZER
41. TURRET
42. AN/APG-32 ANTENNA
43. GYRO DRIVE UNIT
44. RESOLVER

LEFT-UPPER AFT TURRET
1. YOKE GUN SIGHT
2. CONTROL PANEL
3. THYRATRON CONTROLLER
4. COMPUTER
5. GUN SYNCHRONIZER
6. JUNCTION BOX
7. TURRET
8. RESOLVER
9. FREQUENCY CONVERTER ⚠

RIGHT-UPPER AFT TURRET
10. YOKE GUN SIGHT
11. CONTROL PANEL
12. THYRATRON CONTROLLER
13. COMPUTER
14. GUN SYNCHRONIZER
15. JUNCTION BOX
16. TURRET
17. RESOLVER
18. FREQUENCY CONVERTER ⚠

LEFT-LOWER AFT TURRET
19. PEDESTAL GUN SIGHT
20. CONTROL PANEL
21. THYRATRON CONTROLLER
22. COMPUTER
23. JUNCTION BOX
24. GUN SYNCHRONIZER
25. TURRET
26. RESOLVER

RIGHT-LOWER AFT TURRET
27. PEDESTAL GUN SIGHT
28. CONTROL PANEL
29. THYRATRON CONTROLLER
30. COMPUTER
31. JUNCTION BOX
32. GUN SYNCHRONIZER
33. TURRET
34. RESOLVER

⚠ ALSO USED WITH TAIL AND RIGHT LOWER AFT TURRET
⚠ ALSO USED WITH LEFT LOWER AFT TURRET

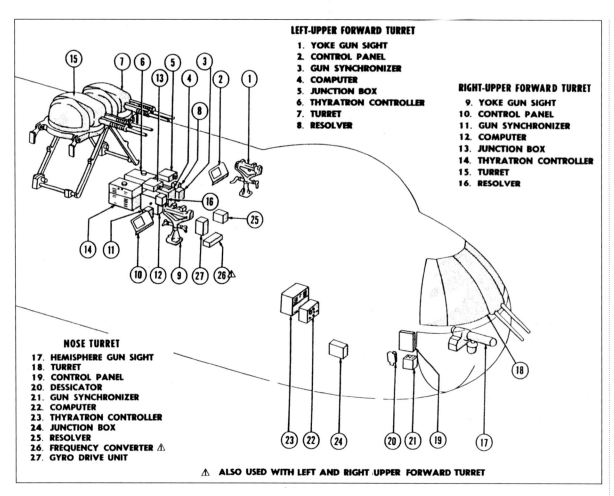

LEFT-UPPER FORWARD TURRET

1. YOKE GUN SIGHT
2. CONTROL PANEL
3. GUN SYNCHRONIZER
4. COMPUTER
5. JUNCTION BOX
6. THYRATRON CONTROLLER
7. TURRET
8. RESOLVER

RIGHT-UPPER FORWARD TURRET

9. YOKE GUN SIGHT
10. CONTROL PANEL
11. GUN SYNCHRONIZER
12. COMPUTER
13. JUNCTION BOX
14. THYRATRON CONTROLLER
15. TURRET
16. RESOLVER

NOSE TURRET

17. HEMISPHERE GUN SIGHT
18. TURRET
19. CONTROL PANEL
20. DESSICATOR
21. GUN SYNCHRONIZER
22. COMPUTER
23. THYRATRON CONTROLLER
24. JUNCTION BOX
25. RESOLVER
26. FREQUENCY CONVERTER ⚠
27. GYRO DRIVE UNIT

⚠ ALSO USED WITH LEFT AND RIGHT UPPER FORWARD TURRET

LEFT: *Defensive armament in the nose and left and right upper turret positions with sights, synchronisers, and control panels.* Convair

turret enclosures were unpressurised, but they were accessible to the crew during flight. The retractable turrets could be operated manually if required with a flush panel sliding down inside the fuselage. The gun firing system had an interrupter gear to inhibit firing during slewed angles threatening propeller tips, the vertical fin and the wings or parts of the fuselage housing crew members.

The weight of each gun was around 100lb (45kg), and they were 77.7in (197cm) in length of which 52.5in (133cm) was the barrel. Each gun had a muzzle velocity of 2,730ft/sec (832m/sec). The nose turret had 800 rounds of ammunition, with 400 rounds in each of two boxes, while the other guns had 1,200 rounds, 600 in each box. There were four different types of ammunition. The M97 was a high-explosive incendiary round, the M62 being a standard incendiary, the AP-1 was an armour-piercing round, and the AP-T was armour-piercing with tracer. In addition to an M95 target practice round there was also a drill-round used for practicing loading and general handling of ammunition and gun in an inactive mode,

After evaluating a wide range of radio-controlled turret (RCT) designs, General Electric developed and manufactured the defensive armament and the control system, the B-36 being the last USAF aircraft to have them.

RCTs had seen extensive application with the B-29, the A-26, and the P-61 but the full hemispheric defence built in to the B-36 was as much a recognition of its lone role as it was an acknowledgement that friendly fighters would be implausible defence escorts given the range of this aircraft.

The fire control system inherited several operational schemes developed for the B-29 and its successor, the B-50, but it had less authority over options.

It could not pass control of turrets between gunners; their operation being shared with the bombardier for control of the forward upper turret. The central station fire controller in the upper bubble sighting station controlled the aft upper turret and had secondary control over the upper forward turret.

Unlike the B-29 and B-50, which had a manned tail turret and upper and lower turrets on the centreline for 360° movement in azimuth and 90°

BELOW: *A nose turret ammunition loading inspection with trailing feed belts at left. AFHRA via Dennis Jenkins*

RIGHT: *The location and related equipment for the nose sight in the forward station. Via Dennis Jenkins*

in elevation, the B-36 turrets were offset to port and starboard with only nose and tail turrets on the centreline. There had been no plan for those earlier aircraft to have manned retractable cannon turrets and weighty multi-gun unmanned central retractable turrets, the arrangement instead being simpler and with lighter 20mm cannon, the mounts for which could be folded down inside the fuselage to reduce drag.

There were fundamental disadvantages to this, in that each sighting station had a dedicated turret and could not be transferred should one be disabled. It also prevented a single gunner from bringing more than a pair of 20mm cannon to bear on a single target. In theory however, six guns operated by three gunners could bring fire to bear on a single target approaching from either flank. Moreover, because there were parallel intercommunication connections, the gunners could throw targets verbally to each other without interference between the communication sets connecting the rest of the crew.

Other advantages included the relatively close proximity of gunners to their turrets, a maximum distance of 11ft (3.35m), eliminating the parallax problems. And because each sighting station had its dedicated control computer, avoiding the need to link them together, wiring was reduced, and the electronics of the fire control system were made simpler. As noted, there had been considerable debate surrounding selection of the guns employed, 20mm cannon being felt sufficient to bring down an attacking fighter. Had the stations been interconnected, the great distance between the fore and aft compartments with their dedicated sighting stations would have made the parallax problem almost insurmountable.

BELOW: *Nose gun turret installation with ammunition feed trays and storage boxes. Via Dennis Jenkins*

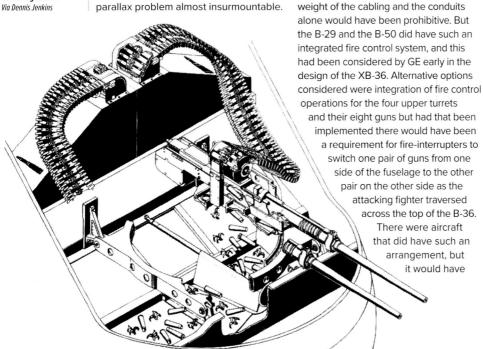

1. **Gunner's Control Panel**
2. **Interphone Control**
3. **Oxygen Controls**

In all, with the B-36's eight sighting stations, seven visual and one radar, there were three more than on the B-29. Had all the stations been interlinked, the sheer weight of the cabling and the conduits alone would have been prohibitive. But the B-29 and the B-50 did have such an integrated fire control system, and this had been considered by GE early in the design of the XB-36. Alternative options considered were integration of fire control operations for the four upper turrets and their eight guns but had that been implemented there would have been a requirement for fire-interrupters to switch one pair of guns from one side of the fuselage to the other pair on the other side as the attacking fighter traversed across the top of the B-36. There were aircraft that did have such an arrangement, but it would have

added complexity when a simpler solution was available offering less weight. However, one peculiarity prevented all four upper turrets from linking with all four sighting stations: the long fuselage tended to flex in turbulent air and had a single interlink been in place that would have prevented proper alignment of the fore and aft upper turrets. This factor alone also influenced the bomb-aiming equipment.

Fault Proofing

There was value in studying the potential performance capabilities of fighters from countries the United States might be called upon to fight. Only in that way could the viability of the B-36 defensive armament be assessed against real-world challenges in the sky. As noted, some of that learning came from B-17 missions over Nazi-occupied Europe, but the B-29 operations against Japanese fighters were also studied in depth. The advanced gunnery and fire-control equipment on that aircraft was a valued learning curve for both the USAAF and the manufacturers for deciding how to configure the B-36.

From the outset, it was recognised that defensive armament on such an aircraft would prove problematic and the first steps to provide improvements began when the US Air Force convened a conference at headquarters on July 21, 1949, to evaluate tests which had been conducted at SAC and at the Air Force Air Proving Ground Command. It was agreed that the configuration of the fire control system for the defensive armament was not fit for operational use and that the highest priority had to be attached to elimination of deficiencies.

Reports came in during August which appeared to show an even worse situation than had been stated at the conference and that a deadline of January 1950 for finding a solution would be missed. Three aircraft were assigned to evaluate fixes, one for Air Materiel Command, one at SAC and one at the Air Force Proving Ground at Eglin AFB, Florida. In September 1949, an RB-36D (44-92058) was assigned to continuous evaluation and test and by May 1950 this activity had found six major and 74 minor changes which would be required for the GE fire control system, but all this did was solve a fire dispersion issue.

Gunnery problems were pursued through increased air firing trials, but they were brought to a halt in September when the deficiencies were judged to be a danger to "life and property." After some caustic and acerbic remarks from the senior command at SAC to news that 91

gunnery deficiencies had been identified, fresh trials on October 25, 1949, were conducted on a B-36B (44-92042) from the 11th BG/7th BW/26th BS, modified to carry a Vitarama movie camera system in place of the right-hand 20mm tail gun. In November, an initial flight at 25,000ft (7,620m) took place over the Eglin AFB range with evaluations made against simulated attacks from F-80s out of Eglin. Two stern attacks were made but the APG-3 gun-laying radar failed, and the radar drive dish became inoperative.

Additional APG-3 tests were conducted by this aircraft where a total of 30 simulated firing passes were made by F-80 and F-82 fighters. These tests moved to Carswell AFB using F-82 Twin Mustang fighters from Bergstrom AFB, Texas, against a B-36D (49-2653) from the 11th BW in September 1950. They were inconclusive and GE concentrated on improving the tail radar but both APG-3 and the newer APG-32 had limitations in which they were unable to search and track at the same time. Once locked on, the radar was unable to search for another target until lock on the initial target was broken.

Effectively the product of a crash programme and a set of modified elements which were tried out first on a B-36D (49-2647) and subsequent D-series and E-series aircraft, the US Air Force afforded GE unlimited overtime and Convair began to install new AN/APG-32 radars in the B-36D. The new

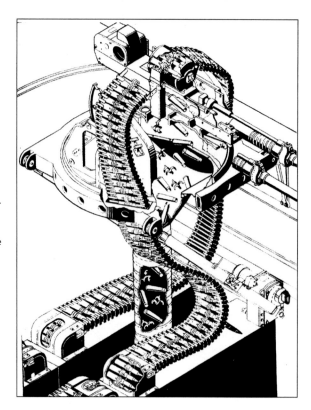

defensive suite carried the series number 2CFR87C1 and when this was installed a significant improvement was immediately apparent. It carried an electronic unit ensuring continuous high-speed output, replacing the electromechanical computer, and it had gyroscope measuring circuits, programmable attack features, and a

ABOVE: *An arrangement drawing for one of the two upper turret ammunition feed trays.* Convair

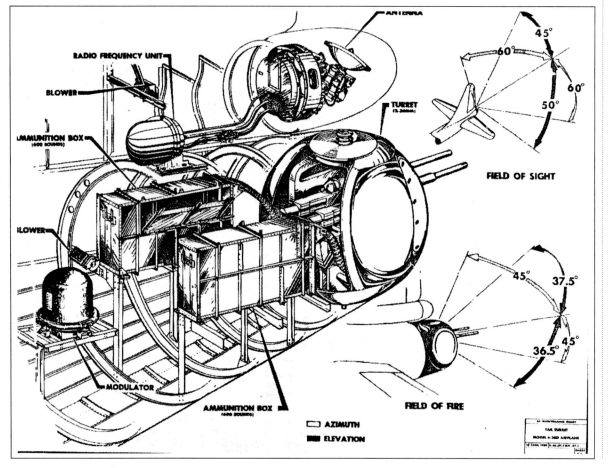

LEFT: *Cone fire maps for the tail turret guns with equipment locations and ammunition feed boxes.* Convair

RIGHT: *Twin guns in the tail showing the ammunition trays and feeder lines.* Convair

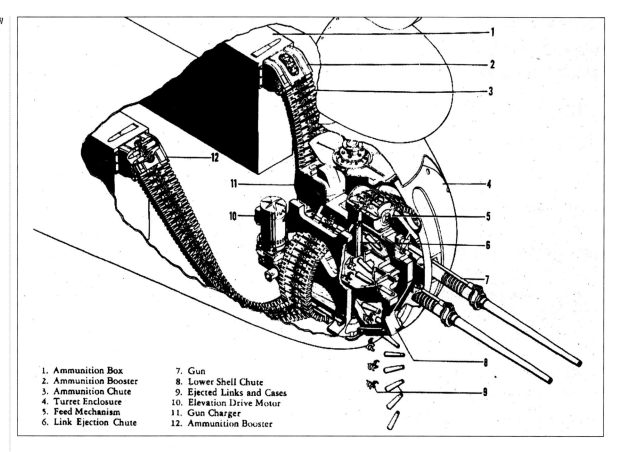

1. Ammunition Box
2. Ammunition Booster
3. Ammunition Chute
4. Turret Enclosure
5. Feed Mechanism
6. Link Ejection Chute
7. Gun
8. Lower Shell Chute
9. Ejected Links and Cases
10. Elevation Drive Motor
11. Gun Charger
12. Ammunition Booster

BELOW: *Looking aft from the top of the forward pressurised compartment glazing, the astrodome on a B-36B.* Via Dennis Jenkins

better construction than the 2CFR87 it replaced.

A partial solution was sought in early 1950 by retrofitting a second radar, the AN/APG-41 and an integrated APG-4 and -31 which became the XAPG-42, effectively a dual set of coupled APG-32s with a dedicated radar display screen and this had the ability to simultaneously search and track, one of the radars locking on to the highest threat and the other searching for new threats. The integrated unit was believed to be simpler to produce and easier to operate and a schedule was set for the first unit to be retrofitted in August 1951. It became standard on a B-52H (5105742) and subsequent production aircraft.

The sixth and final B-36 armament conference was held on June 28, 1950, but not because all the problems

had been solved. Rather, the levels of problem-chasing and the provision of solution paths had been found acceptable and it was decided that no more conferences would be held unless major, unanticipated problems arose. Between May 1 and June 28, fire-control effectiveness had been identified as 62%, far below the required 90% level set by the air force but nothing more could be had from the conferences.

Problems continually appeared to upset reliability levels. Ammunition feed mechanisms jammed, turret power failures froze restricting the movement, feed chutes broke, and the ammunition extractors failed while the occasional human error all accounted for a persistent set of causes. Only long after the B-36 had retired did it become apparent that the training the gunner orientation programme had provided was largely responsible for many of the failures: gunners were given instruction, but not allowed to handle the equipment until in flight, errors in training regimes which became apparent within the programme as both SAC and the operations personnel learned from these avoidable errors.

In 1950 the APG-30 ranging radar was added to all the sighting stations, with a gunner assigned to the remotely-controlled tail turret and it was suggested that the 20mm cannon be replaced by .50 calibre guns in all turrets. The tail turret was supposed to be a hemispheric sight, similar to that in the nose, with a four-gun, .50

calibre wide-angle turret which had been designed for the XB-54. The reconfiguration of turret assignments stemmed from tests that indicated most attacks would come from the stern and that this was where the defensive priority should be allocated. Hence, the tail turret received the most attention. It was this that prompted SAC to move toward switching all guns to .50 calibre.

The weight of the defensive armament consisted of 6,143lb (2,746kg) in the GE turrets, sights and computers and US Air Force equipment including guns and synchronisers, etc. Equipment provided by Convair weighed in at 1,149lb (521kg) while armour plating added a further 731lb (331kg). This was broken down into turrets and sighting station weights of 842lb (382kg) for the nose turret, 1,775lb (805kg) for the upper forward turret, 1,815lb (823kg) for the aft upper, 1,696lb (769kg) for the aft lower and 1,164lb (528kg) for the tail turret.

Intelligence information was acquired indicating that the more capable MiG-17 operated by the Russians was closing the gap between what Soviet fighters could reach in altitude and the operating ceiling of the B-36. Through the Featherweight programme which readers can find in the next chapter, the operating altitude of the Peacemaker outpaced the effective ceiling of the MiG fighters, but only for a while although judicious use of the J47 jet engines proved effective. Nevertheless, by the end of 1951 the US Air Force was already concerned about the encroaching vulnerability of the B-36.

Service Life

The B-36 served with the US Air Force for 10 years, forming the atomic deterrent wielded by Strategic Air Command, and participating in the greatest transformation of air power in the history of military aviation.

Moving from a national deterrent force to an instrument for strategic strike carrying the most powerful weapons ever devised, the B-36 came to Strategic Air Command in the year that the organisation moved its headquarters from Andrews AFB, Maryland, to Offutt AFB, Nebraska, officially moving across from November 9, 1948. In this year there were 35 B-36 aircraft on line, but that means very little. The categorisation of aircraft on strength can vary from numbered air force to group and to squadron and should be viewed with caution. Definition of 'strength' in the active inventory usually indicates a date in which aircraft were accredited to a unit or air force. As is the case with many new types, this was no clear indication of an operational capability. Not all of those on strength were available for operational integration, either for flight planning or assigned missions in time of conflict.

The first B-36A (44-92004) arrived on June 26, 1948, and went to the 7th BG at Carswell AFB. From this date the Very Heavy Bombers (B-29 and B-50) became Medium Bombers, and the B-36 was re-designated as a Heavy Bomber. In time, the B-47 replaced the B-29/B-50 types, and the B-52 replaced the B-36. Challenged by time-consuming integration and shakedown tasks with the B-36, SAC was also solving manpower, management, and expansion problems as well as trying to achieve credible and accurate simulated bombing capabilities.

Notionally, in 1949, SAC had 36 B-36s on strength, a year in which the US Air Force placed top priority on equipping SAC and standing it up as the strategic deterrent stick of the United States. Training reached high levels of commitment and intensity and recruitment was a major driving force in building up personnel from 51,965 the previous year to 71,490 by the end of 1949. Emphasis was still on the B-29/B-50 types, and personnel were on a pseudo war-footing, with high stress levels and a driving imperative to strengthen the deterrent arm, reacting to a worsening global crisis epitomised by the Berlin blockade, which began on June 24, 1948, and ended on May 12, 1949.

On March 12, 1949, the B-36 began to flex its muscles, with a record flight of 9,600 miles (15,446km) by an aircraft of the 7th Bomb Group, completed in 49 hours 37 minutes, starting, and finishing at Fort Worth using a crew of 12 piloted by Captain Roy Showalter. The first bombing competition involving the B-36 took place October 3-7 with a 28th BG aircraft winning the individual crew trophy. Nevertheless, the build-up of aircraft on strength was slow due to the ponderous and simultaneous preparation of the aircraft, incorporating both design and development with production in the flawed concept of 'concurrency' explored in earlier chapters.

In 1950, SAC boasted 38 B-36 bombers and 20 RB-36 types on strength with personnel now at 85,473 and a total of 962 aircraft, up from 837 in 1948 and 868 in 1949. This was the first year of the Korean War, but the

BELOW: *A line of RB-36H reconnaissance aircraft, with 52-1384 in the foreground on the maintenance line at Fort Worth, nose areas covered by Sun screens. Via Dennis Jenkins*

B-36 did not participate, bombing operations in theatre being handled by B-29 and B-50 units. But it was in 1950 that the B-36 began to bed in and serve as a seminal and polarising factor for SAC in the more balanced organisation it was becoming. Of only incidental relevance, this was also the year the RB-45 entered service with the 91st SRS at Barksdale AFB, Louisiana, with reconnaissance becoming an accelerating priority for the air force and for SAC in particular.

The big jump in the B-36 inventory came in 1951 when SAC had 163 on strength, of which 65 were reconnaissance variants, the personnel level had jumped to 144,525 and a total force of 1,186 aircraft were listed for the command. During that year, two wings operated the B-36 with a third transitioning from the B-29s. On January 16, six aircraft of the 7th BW, Carswell AFB, flew to Lakenheath, England, giving British citizens their first look at the B-36, returning four days later. On December 3, six B-36s of the 11th BW arrived at Sidi Slimane after a non-stop flight from the United States during the first visit by these aircraft to French Morocco. They returned five days later.

The sustained expansion of SAC saw 268 B-36s on strength in 1952 in a total inventory of 1,830 aircraft, the command growing a fourth wing of Convair bombers and a third and fourth wing of reconnaissance variants. Held over October 13 to 18, four B-36 wings joined 10 B-29 and five B-50 wings in the fourth annual bombing competition out of Davis-Monthan

AFB, Arizona, with the B-36s operating out of Walker AFB, New Mexico. Following this, the SAC reconnaissance and navigation competition was held October 23 to November 1, involving B-36 aircraft from Rapid City AFB, South Dakota, forming two of the four wings competing. The highest score was achieved by the 28th SRS/8th AF and recipient of the P T Cullen Award which had been named after Brig Gen Paul T Cullen who had been killed in a C-124 crash on March 23, 1951.

The following year SAC stood up 322 B-36s of which 137 were reconnaissance variants with four wings and 185 were bombers in six wings. Action in the Korean War ceased on July 27, 1953, when an armistice was signed by both sides. During August and September, the 92nd BW conducted the first mass B-36 flight to the Far East with visits to Japan, Okinawa, and Guam, appropriately named 'Big Stick' in a demonstration of the US commitment to maintaining peace in the region. This was the first appearance of the B-36 in that area and underscored the intention to use whatever force was necessary to shut down a resurgence of violence.

The fifth annual bombing competition held from October 25 to 31 was joined by four B-36 wings alongside four B-50 and two B-29 wings out of Walker AFB. But the writing was on the wall when seven B-47 wings out of David-Monthan AFB joined the competition, leveraging the advent of an all-jet bomber force. Nevertheless, four B-36 wings joined one RB-50 wing, an RB-29 wing and, uniquely, one YRB-47 wing in the

annual reconnaissance competition out of Ellsworth AFB, South Dakota, held from October 18 to 27. An RB-36 from the 15th AF won the Cullen award.

B-36 strength reached its peak in 1954 with 209 bombers and 133 reconnaissance variants, a total of 342 in a total SAC inventory of 2,640 aircraft, of which 795 were medium B-47 bombers. The first B-36 rotation to Guam occurred on October 15-16, when the 92nd BW stationed at Fairchild AFB, Washington, deployed to Andersen AFB on a 90-day training visit. This marked the first time a complete B-36 wing deployed to an overseas base. From June 16 the four B-36 reconnaissance wings were shifted to a bombing role as their primary mission, with reconnaissance duties retained as a secondary capability.

The B-36s dominated the six events in the reconnaissance and navigation competition held August 8-14 and six B-36 wings from Walker AFB joined the annual bombing competition on August 23-29, two crews being permitted from each wing joining the 15 B-47 wings and two B-50 wings. Testament to the refinement of their capabilities, the B-36s took the top three placings in both the bombing and the reconnaissance competitions, significantly outclassing the B-47s which had yet to demonstrate an equivalent bombing capability.

Mixed Abilities

This was a time of tremendous growth and overall expansion in SAC, with 142,000 air refuelling hook-ups and over 3,400 transatlantic and transpacific

All-jet bombers could achieve higher speeds and greater altitude and the sustained search for those performance assets pushed the air force toward supersonic bombers and projects such as the 1952 contract for the B-58 Hustler and the 1955 study leading to the B-70 Valkyrie programme, both of which would fail to deliver precisely what the USAF wanted.

Within SAC, a determination to improve the way crews could handle the troublesome defensive armament had already resulted in a series of tests to discover the root cause of the problems and it was defined by potential obstacles in crew training, inadequate maintenance, and poor equipment design. Consequently, 'Test Fire' was run as an operational exercise from August 29 to December 9, 1952, using RB-36Ds from the 28th SRW and effectively demonstrating that the defensive system was inadequate. Early in 1953 the air force ran the 'Hit More' programme which brought together

ABOVE: *RB-36D 49-2688 displays the different surface reflectivity of the dull magnesium panels in this evocative shot of the aircraft in flight.* Via Dennis Jenkins

LEFT: *A snow-covered Loring Air Force Base, northeastern Maine, with five B-36s and four KC-97K cargo-tankers.* USAF

BELOW: *Ground crew, air crew and a Convair engineer chat about maintenance issues in front of B-36B 44-92032.* USAF

crossings in 1954. Air-to-air refuelling erased the unique range advantage of the B-36, but one advantage claimed for the B-36 was its defensive armament, all but eliminated on the fast B-47s and the B-52s, the latter of which would appear in service during the following year.

The plausibility of fighter escorts along part of a bombing flight path were proposed as being more readily available by the same process of in-flight refuelling. The bombers and fighter fraternities, two competing camps of influence in US Air Force procurement strategy, fought for ways to release the bombers from the early concept of fighter escort. There were some within the bomber camp who sought high performance in new aircraft, providing high speed and high altitude immunity from interception while some analysts within the fighter fraternity sought expanded escort roles. The majority, however, saw the fighter role as one based around interception and attack rather than escort and defensive roles.

Nevertheless, the operating experience with the B-36 and a parallel analogue in the B-47 and the B-52

recognised the seminal shift in doctrinal thinking about the way bombers and fighters should be used. With a very high weight penalty, the defensive armament on the B-36 was justified by the aircraft's relatively slow speed.

ABOVE: *Bombing up a B-36 with conventional munitions with the loading truck and hoist.* Via Dennis Jenkins

operational tests by the service with engineers from Convair and General Electric to propose a solution.

This series of tests involved one B-36B converted to a D-series (44-92054), retained as a test aircraft for its service life until retired in September 1957 after 244 flights totalling 1,600 hours. It fired a quarter million rounds of 20mm ammunition and was subject to major modifications including the addition of a radome installed in its nose to evaluate a range of air-defence radar systems and also several antenna and other structures for electronic counter-measures. So successful were these tests that it was loaned out for evaluation of other aircraft systems, including a suite of equipment for the Convair B-58, also becoming the prototype for the R-4360-53 engine.

Test Fire and Hit More had used six B-36Ds modified by GE, Convair, and the air force to provide a real-world assessment of the in-flight performance of defensive armament. Carrying numerous minor modifications, a more rigorous training programme, and with detailed attention to the equipment, the performance of the armament system began to significantly improve. It demonstrated that with effective crew training, resilient attention to the robust maintenance of the equipment, and focused concentration on operational procedures, the defensive suite could be made to work quite effectively.

During this time, many crew members were called to duty from reserve status in civilian life but former gunners, bombardiers, navigators, and flight engineers returning to the air force had missed a generation of development and technological advances since their last service during World War Two. Much of the problem faced by SAC was due to this alone, many crew members

RIGHT: *This panel was to be used for releasing atomic bombs from bays one and four on selected targets, additional panels being fitted when bombs were to be dropped from bays two and three.* NARA

openly confessing to be perplexed over the sophistication of the new electronic operating systems and the associated computers. Training was good, effective, and getting better, but it was not adapted to the unusual position in which these men found themselves. However, once employed, corrective procedures paid dividends, but the challenges remained as the air force expanded in the wake of global threats.

In 1955, as the SAC inventory soared to 3,068 aircraft, of which 338 were B-36s (205 bombers and 133 reconnaissance types). The B-47 medium bomber continued to dominate the inventory with 1,086 listed together with the first 18 B-52s on strength. The re-designation of RB-36 reconnaissance wings continued with a further four allocated as bomber wings on October 1, retaining some reconnaissance capability but now as

a secondary role. While much of the heavy-lift to overseas bases was being taken up by B-47 wings, rotating to Lakenheath, Upper Heyford, Fairford, Mildenhall and Brize Norton in England, B-36 wings were also deployed to Nouasseur Air Base, French Morocco, to Burtonwood and Upper Heyford in England and Andersen AFB, Guam.

As the B-50 was at the terminal end of its phase-out plan, only B-47s and B-36s were available for the seventh bombing competition held August 24 to 30, with 10 B-36s wings each putting up two crews from Fairchild AFB, Washington. The B-47s showed tremendous improvement in both bombing and navigation and the 15th AF's 320th BW won the Fairchild Trophy. As all the RB-36s had been formally re-designated as bomber wings, only five RB-47 wings could compete in the second series of events, the reconnaissance and navigation competition which was held from September 24 to 30.

In 1956, while the number of SAC personnel reached 217,279 officers, airmen, and civilians and the total tactical inventory reached 3,218 aircraft of all types, the B-36 fleet was reduced to 247 as combined bomber and reconnaissance aircraft, in that order of priority. But this was also the year the last B-47 was delivered, the inventory reaching 1,560. Of 42 wings competing in the bombing, navigation and reconnaissance competition held August 24-30, only eight B-36 wings participated. This time the B-36s got their own back on the B-47s, beating the latter to the Fairchild Trophy, won by an aircraft from the 2nd AF, 11th BW.

Responding to concerns that Soviet ICBM deployment was imminent, SAC began to transition toward a one-third ground alert operation so that a significant part of the retaliatory

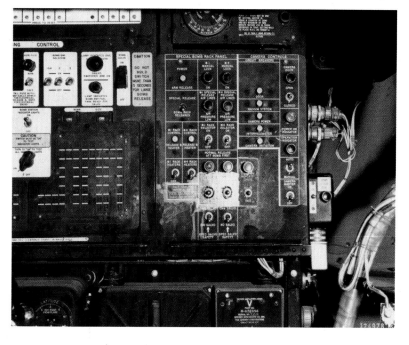

Featherweight Bombers

During the period in which it served, increasing Cold War tensions drew the B-36 in to evolving plans for quick response and rapid strike capability in the event of attack. Emerging concerns about the strength of Soviet air and missile forces generated conflicting concerns: that a new generation of Russian bombers and attack aircraft could threaten North American air defences, and that ICBMs could take out many vital bases and their command and control facilities with very little warning.

It was no longer possible to rely on foreign bases for pre-attack staging, as had been the case immediately after World War Two; these could be destroyed long before the B-36s got there from the United States. Moreover, foreign bases were costly to maintain, requiring valuable stores and logistical support along with manpower and an amenable political regime. The Pentagon was becoming increasingly concerned over the cost and dubious strategic advantage in overseas bases and the dilemma of substantive requirements for airborne operations fed into that concern. But there were concerns too about the ability of the B-36 to reach assigned targets within the Soviet sphere of influence.

Calculations on flight paths and range showed that operations from only one base, at Limestone AFB, Maine, could support direct operations from CONUS (Continental United States) to deep inside the USSR where most of the targets were located. A major problem was the revised doctrine of how to wage a global war involving nuclear weapons which went in parallel to the determination that, with lightweight thermonuclear devices now becoming available, each aircraft would have

LEFT AND BELOW:
Developed over several decades from the 1920s, the Norden bombsight was operated as an electronic tachometer with particular application to strategic bombers in World War Two and early production B-36s. Author's archive

force would be away from airfields vulnerable to a pre-emptive first strike by the time warheads reached their targets. Crews and aircraft would be prepared for immediate take-off so as to get airborne on alert of an attack. But SAC was not equipped for this, and a structural reorganisation was essential to implementing the new strategy.

In 1957, to prepare for placing a third of its active force on ground alert, SAC began the phase out of the KB-29 as well as the B-47, at a time when the B-36 force was in decline, with 127 remaining in a force boasting a total complement of 2,711 aircraft. The annual bombing and reconnaissance competitions were held October 30 to November 6 and 43 bomber wings from Pinecastle AFB, Florida, and Carswell AFB, Texas, participated. Of those, five were B-36 wings which won the crew and wing navigation awards, the B-47 wings winning out over the B-36 each time they competed in the bombing competition.

The transition to one-third ground alert accelerated through 1958, an adaptation which brought about considerable change to the organisational infrastructure of SAC, which now had a personnel strength of 258,703 and 3,031 aircraft, including

the last 22 B-36 bombers on strength. In this year, the last two B-36 crews to participate in a bombing competition, October 13-18, participated out of Carswell AFB but the B-47 crews dominated the event, and the operational life of the B-36 was over.

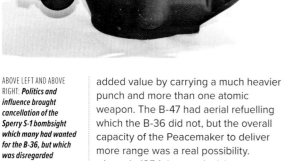

ABOVE LEFT AND ABOVE RIGHT: *Politics and influence brought cancellation of the Sperry S-1 bombsight which many had wanted for the B-36, but which was disregarded despite claims that it was superior to the Norden equipment.*
Author's archive

added value by carrying a much heavier punch and more than one atomic weapon. The B-47 had aerial refuelling which the B-36 did not, but the overall capacity of the Peacemaker to deliver more range was a real possibility.

In early 1954, just as decisions were being made about the overall configuration of SAC after the B-36 was retired and a new generation of weapons became available, a strongly contested debate began to develop over the balance between missiles and manned aircraft. It introduced the

phrase 'push-button warfare' from those already involved in the balance of procurement, seeking efficiencies through unmanned strike systems and fewer maintenance and support personnel than were required to operate aircraft.

Entering this debate were General Bernard Schriever, who supported a greater reliance on rockets and missiles, and General Curtis LeMay favouring the manned strategic bomber, a weapon system that was flexible in operational roles and which could be target-adapted

and called back or redirected. Schriever was the architect of the air force missile programmes and from 1954 would receive a mandate to transition the air force to a dual-functional arm of the USAF operating both manned and unmanned weapons. Conversely, as a 'bomber pilot's pilot', LeMay saw the logic of having a rapid-response missile arsenal, but not at the expense of the manned intruder with all the advantages that held.

To revitalise the role of the manned penetrating bomber and to give the

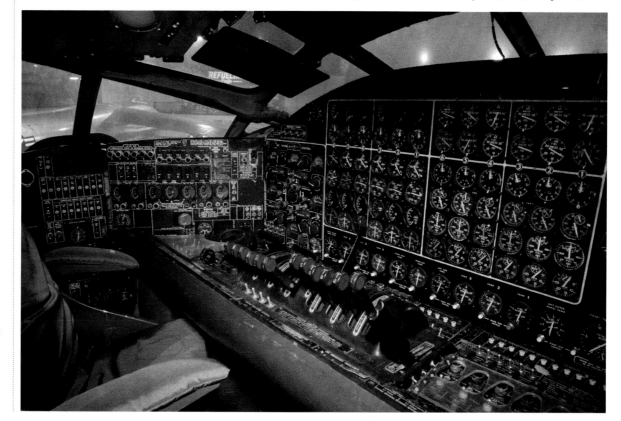

RIGHT: *The B-36H introduced significant changes to the rear of the forward pressurised crew compartment with an additional seat for a second flight engineer, increasing crew effectiveness and personal comfort.*
Via Dennis Jenkins

top of the cockpit. By eliminating most of the guns, two crew members could be stood down but because insulation would be taken out, heated flight suits would be provided, equipped with integral communications sets; weight saving raised the ceiling which would add to crew discomfort without those new suits.

Configuration 3 Featherweight measures reduced weight by 15,000lb (6,804kg) and that increased the range by 25-40% over Configuration 2 reductions, depending on the specific model. Overall, by reducing drag and lightening the airframe, the top speed of the B-36D was increased to 418mph (672kph) and for the B-36H to 423mph (680kph). But the greatest operational advantage carried the rated ceiling to 47,000ft (14,325m) and to more than 50,000ft (15,240m) on some flights, testified to by the crew on several test missions. Several crews swore they achieved 55,000ft (16,764m).

Configuration 1 changes were never adopted in their entirety but most of those proposed changes were applied at depot level. Configuration 2 changes were adopted universally, and those aircraft carried a (II) suffix to their series identification, such as B-36D (II) or B-36D-II with a similar identification code for the Configuration 3 types (B-36D-III). Rapidly, the entire fleet of aircraft went through the Featherweight programme but there were other, more subtle changes. They were each given improved, and enhanced, support for the thermonuclear role and ECM equipment was relocated from bomb bay four to the aft fuselage while some aircraft had a modified bombardier's scope.

From June 16, 1954, the shift back to a bomber priority for the

LEFT: The second flight engineer seat on the B-36H and J series was located to the right (facing aft) of the original position on the starboard side. Note that the flight engineers still had the jet engine throttle levers.
Via Dennis Jenkins

LEFT: The radio operator's position was supported by more advanced equipment, replacing contingency apparatus such as a Morse code key for sending messages via telegraph.
Via Dennis Jenkins

BELOW: The radar/ bombardier's position on the B-36H with the bombsight at lower left incorporating the Farrand Y-3 periscope.
Via Dennis Jenkins

B-36 better performance, three weight reduction concepts were implemented for the B-36 under the Featherweight programme. In Configuration 1, immediately prior to their use on real-world bombing missions, all extraneous equipment would be removed, including all the retractable turrets, the auxiliary bomb racks for conventional bombs, and the crew comfort upgrades already introduced on production aircraft.

Configuration 2 would repeat much of the above but also take out unnecessary ECM equipment, external drag-inducing protuberances, with periscopes and high altitude equipment added in addition to flush covers for all sighting blisters. These changes could be carried out at depot level and shaved 4,800lb (2,177kg) from the weight of an operational aircraft. Tests showed that Category 2 weight-shaving increased range by 25% with guns fitted and to 39% without defensive armament.

Configuration 3 was the most stringent weight reduction programme proposed, involving complete removal of all defensive armament, but leaving the tail turret and upper and lower aft sighting blisters in place. These could be replaced with Plexiglass and the lower

blisters were a convenient location for engineers to check for leaks. Chaff dispensers would be retained, with ECM equipment upgraded with lighter, and improved, derivative equipment.

Crew comfort equipment would also be removed as would the astrodome on

ABOVE: *B-36s reach the end of the line, awaiting their fate at AMARC (the Aircraft Maintenance and Regeneration Center) in Tucson, Arizona, during 1958.* Author's archive

B-36 Strategic Air Command Units 1948-1958				
Air Force	Wing	Squadron	Base	Dates
2nd	72nd	60th SRS; 301st SRS	Ramey AFB Puerto Rico	October 1952-January 1959
8th	6th BW	24th BS; 39th BS; 40th BS	Walker AFB New Mexico	August 1952–August 1957
	7th BW	9th BS; 436th BS; 492nd BS	Carswell AFB Texas	June 1948–May 1958
	11th BW	26th BS; 42nd BS; 98th BS	Carswell AFB Texas	December 1948-December 1957
	28th SRW	77th SRS; 717th SRS; 718th SRS	Ellsworth AFB South Dakota	May 1949-April 1950
	47th BW	69th BS; 70th BS; 75th BS	Loring AFB Maine	April 1953-September 1956
15th	92nd BW	325th BS; 326th BS; 327th BS	Fairchild AFB Washington	July 1951-March 1956
	95th BW	334th BS; 335th BS; 336th BS	Biggs AFB Texas	August 1953-February 1959
	5th SRW	5th SRS; 31st SRS; 72nd SRS	Fairfield-Suisun AFB California	January 1951-September 1958
	9th SRW	1st BS	Fairfield-Suisun AFB California	May 1949-April 1950
	90th SRW	346th SRS; 347th SRS; 348th SRS	Fairchild AFB Washington	August 1951-September 1956

B-36 recognised the increasingly important role the B-47 was playing in reconnaissance and the Featherweight programme acknowledged that, although there was some concern on SAC's part for eliminating two crew members. On October 1, 1955, all RB-36 reconnaissance wings were re-designated heavy-bombardment wings but in reality, reconnaissance duties were still a very ready option.

BELOW: *Seen at the Boeing Wichita site in 1951, the B-47 saw service along with the B-36, a portent of the all-jet bomber force to come.* USAF

The Featherweight aircraft modification programme began in February 1954, with the final converted aircraft returned for operations six months later, the last bomber being delivered in November followed by the last modified RB-36 in May 1955. Anti-flash paint was applied from late 1954 when the aircraft entered scheduled modification cycles. However, indicative of the pace of technological change, the B-36 was to spend more time in modification and maintenance than any other aircraft in the US Air Force inventory.

In mid-1953 SAC and Convair had entered into rolling modification and modernisation cycles which would see every B-36 going through a commonality update and improvement programme, in parallel to the Featherweight treatment. Known as the Specialised Aircraft Maintenance (SAM) scheme, an RB-36E (42-13571, the original YB-36) was the first aircraft to enter the cycle with the last aircraft (52-2216) redelivered back to SAC on April 29, 1957. This process required 59 days per aircraft and 38 maintenance docks in work simultaneously on 13 aircraft a month.

Much has been made of the dual role performed by the B-36, designed, and developed as a strategic bomber but employed in great numbers for reconnaissance purposes which were never envisaged originally. That story is just as fascinating as the prime function for which it was built, as a conventional bomber adapted into SAC's prime atomic and thermonuclear delivery platform.

Reconnaissance Roles

Probing potential threats through denied airspace was not new to the US Air Force but SAC brought a particularly effective advance to that capability.

From the outset, military aircraft had been used primarily for reconnaissance, surveillance, and gun-laying duties. Only later did air combat emerge when spotting-planes had to be brought down, and again when other aircraft could be used to drop bombs. By World War Two, fighting aircraft were equipped to carry out all those other functions too. Intelligence is the key to informing tactical and strategic mission planners about the state of the enemy's war preparations, defences, material assets and fighting capabilities. In a sequence of precedence, the ability to engage the enemy is determined by the logistical supplies available which in turn relies on sound intelligence.

All combatant forces grew their reconnaissance capability around selected aircraft designed specifically for air combat or bombing. General Curtis LeMay was particularly concerned to have all his bombers adapted for reconnaissance duties and this applied to B-29, B-36, B-45, B-47, and B-57 aircraft. Only the B-52 escaped this adopted role without

a designated variant specifically assigned to reconnaissance, largely due to the emergence of dedicated reconnaissance assets including the U-2 and SR-71 at the most exotic end of the range and across to fighters specially adapted for photographic missions.

With its high-altitude and great weight-lifting capability, the operational deployment of the B-36 brought a unique capability to SAC at a time when much information was needed to support target location and mapping across potential enemy territory which had never previously been surveyed in detail. With the deep chill of the Cold War, LeMay was anxious to get as much information as possible about the exact location of key assets materiel to a future war with the Soviet Union and turned to the Peacemaker to achieve some of that objective.

Russia was a largely unmapped country and the US Air Force had to rely on captured Luftwaffe photographs and German maps created before and during Operation Barbarossa in 1941. Many of the Russian maps available in

the West were deliberately incorrect, accurate maps only being available to Soviet government personnel. With the atomic bomb, the US Air Force needed detailed information about ports, industrial facilities, marshalling yards and military bases, frequently misidentified and incorrectly placed in different locations to confuse a potential invader, of which Russia had more than most European countries.

The origin of the B-36 reconnaissance programme dates back to early 1948 when Convair and some specialist reconnaissance camera companies were asked to produce a mock-up of equipment, the first being scrutinised on March 17, 1949, and reviewed by the air force over the next several months. The designations for these aircraft were the RB-36E, these being exclusively reworked A-series aircraft brought to B-series standard, and the RB-36D, which were entirely new-builds. The only significant difference between the two were their origin on the production line and over time all were brought to the D-series standard. In this regard the usual variant suffix letter applied

ABOVE: *An RB-36D (49-2688) with clearly visible magnesium panels presents a striking view of this multi-role behemoth. Note the radome for the search radar in place of the forward underside gun turrets. Via Dennis Jenkins*

ABOVE: *Activated in June 1952, the 72nd SRW operated the RB-36, seen here with its 22-man crew with flight equipment at Ramey Air Force Base, Puerto Rico, in 1954. USAF*

the traditional one of taking pictures from a great height.

Over time, Convair delivered 142 reconnaissance types, around one-third of all B-36 aircraft produced, and it is arguably in that role that the B-36 was of more operational use. Although, the sheer presence of the B-36 as a bomber in the SAC inventory sent a very clear message to the Soviet hierarchy and the freshly minted communist state of the People's Republic of China.

Eyes in the Sky

To adapt the B-36 to a strategic reconnaissance role, substantial modifications were made, with the No.1 bomb bay converted to a 16ft (4.87m) long housing for up to 23 cameras of which 14 were in a pressurised compartment. The No.2 bay would house photo-flash bombs and the pressurised crew access tunnel was modified into two separate sections, a very short one running from the forward compartment to the new pressurised photo compartment, and which did not require a transfer cart, and a second tunnel from the aft end of the photo compartment through three of the four original bomb bays to the aft pressurised section, that section of the tunnel retaining the cart. Bays three and four were modified for containing electronics equipment.

These facilities required the forward and aft bulkheads to be converted into

more to the production lot than to the particulars of a specific variant.

A special board comprising 75 US Air Force officers and civilians, set up to evaluate all new types prior to entering production, examined the reconnaissance variant on November 21, 1949, and in an inspection lasting five days they approved the modifications. The crew complement changed significantly, with roles and

responsibilities altered, the total complement growing from 15 to 22 personnel, additional crew members being assigned to operating the cameras and photographic equipment as well as the electronic reconnaissance systems. By the 1950s, considerable attention was being paid to the identification, location and frequency mapping of radio communications and radar sites and this role was added to

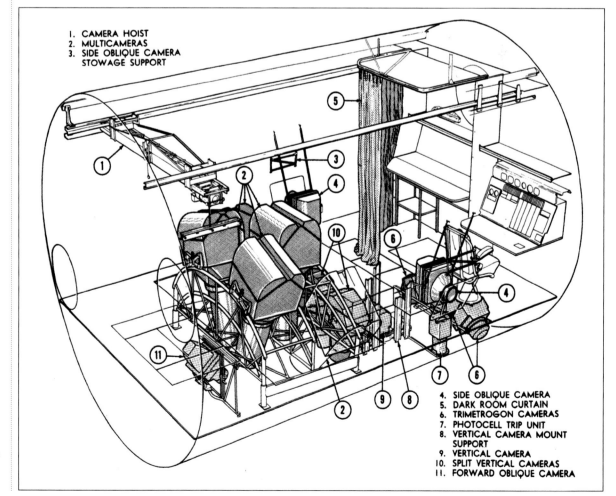

1. CAMERA HOIST
2. MULTICAMERAS
3. SIDE OBLIQUE CAMERA STOWAGE SUPPORT

4. SIDE OBLIQUE CAMERA
5. DARK ROOM CURTAIN
6. TRIMETROGON CAMERAS
7. PHOTOCELL TRIP UNIT
8. VERTICAL CAMERA MOUNT SUPPORT
9. VERTICAL CAMERA
10. SPLIT VERTICAL CAMERAS
11. FORWARD OBLIQUE CAMERA

RIGHT: *The pressurised camera compartment on the RB-36 together with processing booth and light curtain. Convair*

(45kg). These bombs were located in bay No.2 and a photocell trip would expose the film when the flash fired. The remotely controlled cameras would be used in conjunction with determinations of altitude, speed, and settings on the intervalometer, a device which measured brief intervals of time and could trigger exposures at previously set intervals. Two C-1 radarscope cameras were also carried in the photo compartment together with one A-6 movie camera, operated by the photo-navigator located in the forward fuselage.

Initially, the bomb bay positions two and three were covered with a single set of doors, 33.6ft (10.2m) in length, the No.3 bay containing an auxiliary fuel tank or additional flash bombs. No bombs were carried on the reconnaissance versions, permitting removal of the Norden or periscope bomb sights. The No.4 bay supported a single pallet with electronic eavesdropping equipment in external positions where the two aft bomb bays would normally be found. Three large radomes were installed and through these, operators could record and analyse communications and radar signals, allowing identification and frequency mapping of Soviet defence and acquisition radars.

Some degree of weight-reduction was possible, engineers at Convair taking the opportunity to install different bulkheads on each end of the place where the bomb racks would normally be supported. Also, some of the fuselage frames were lightened and changes were made to the wing spar which also helped reduce weight.

Ferret ECM equipment was installed in bay No.4 on all reconnaissance variants with most of the defensive electronics situated in the forward fuselage, as it was for the bomber versions. While the same amount of equipment was retained, when the B-36 was adapted from a bombing role a considerable re-arrangement of location took place,

pressure domes and changes to the bomb bay doors were made together with switching to aluminium for the exterior skin since magnesium could not withstand the pressure cycles. This allowed easy visual identification of the reconnaissance versions, together with the various windows, covered with sliding doors when not in use.

The primary cameras employed were the K-17C, K-22A, K-38, and K-40. There was a facility serving as a darkroom to allow cartridges to be reloaded with new film while the aircraft was still in the air. The maximum complement of cameras had two fixed and five remotely controlled locations, designated as the trimetrogon, vertical, split-vertical,

multi, and forward oblique positions. The trimetrogon is an arrangement of three fixed cameras, one pointing down and two either side of the ground-track at a 30° depression angle (60° from vertical) with overlapping images for stereoscopic views of undulating topography. These were controlled from the photo-navigators station in the nose or from the photographer's station in the photographic compartment.

The two oblique cameras were controlled from their respective positions by switches operated by the photographer. The vertical camera could also be used for night photography when it would be operated in conjunction with 88 T-86 or M46 photo-flash bombs, each weighing 100lb

but the bombardier was replaced with the photo-navigator in the extreme nose who was afforded excellent views of the ground below and to either side, As would be the practice for a bombing run, the pilot handed over control of the aircraft to the photo-navigator who would position the flight path over the desired ground track and steer the aircraft from that point on. He would also operate the cameras. The photographer in the photo compartment was responsible for the film magazines and for changing cassettes as necessary, also controlling the heating and the dehumidifier as well as looking after the technical performance of the cameras.

A New Cold War Chill

Largely unsung, even to this day, was the early start made in the post-war period for obtaining information vital to any preparation for war, such as those discussed from page 34. Initially, it was the B-29 that conducted flights across the Arctic wastes to discover and map land areas which were close to the Soviet Union. Under Operation Nanook, the 46th Squadron (Very Long Range) was set up under SAC and on August 14, 1946, it was authorised to conduct

especially for carrying atom bombs and thermonuclear weapons. Several structural changes were required when the B-36 was reconfigured to a bombing role. The bulkheads for the reconnaissance versions were redesigned and that formed a major part of the structural changes that were useful for the aircraft carrying gravity atom bombs.

Similar modifications were adopted for the weather reconnaissance aircraft, conducting missions to get meteorological data through a weather observer station in the extreme nose. For this role, radio altimeters were attached to the underside of the horizontal tail and associated electronics were installed in the aft pressurised compartment. A probe for measuring barometric pressure, temperature, and humidity was attached to the starboard side of the extreme nose behind the glazed panelling.

An equipment rack for a radiosonde was installed at the operator station for the intermediate frequency ECM operator. The sonde dispenser was mounted to the floor of the centreline in the rear pressurised compartment at the same location as the strike camera

which was a standard installation on the bomber versions. The controls for the sonde were situated in the high-frequency ECM station on the starboard side of the aft compartment and at the lower gunner's blister on the same side of the fuselage.

Flying characteristics of the RB-36 differed little from the bomber version,

Selected performance parameters for RB-36H and RB-36H III

	RB-36H Basic Mission	RB-36H Max Bombs	RB-36H III Basic Mission	RB-36H III Max Bombs
T/O Weight	370,000lb (167,832kg)	370,000lb (167,832kg)	370,000lb (167,832kg)	370,000lb (167,832kg)
Load	5,054lb (2,292kg)	17,838lb (8,091kg)	3,664lb (1,662kg)	16,448lb (7,460kg)
T/O Distance	5,110ft (1,557m)	5,110ft (1,557m)	5,110ft (1,557m)	5,110ft (1,557m)
Climb rate	910ft/min (277m/min)	910ft/min (277m/min)	940ft/min (286m/min)	940ft/min (286m/min)
Max speed	407mph (654kph)	409mph (658kph)	416mph (669kph)	418mph (672kph)
Service ceiling	42,700ft (13,014m)	43,200ft (13,167m)	43,900ft (13,380m)	44,300ft (13,502m)
Combat radius	2,934miles (4,720km)	2,623miles (4,220km)	3,619miles (5,823km)	3,308miles (5,322km)
Landing Weight	204,610lb (92,811kg)	204,710lb (92,856kg)	188,410lb (85,462kg)	188,260lb (85,394kg)
Mission Time	25.3hrs	22.6hrs	29.9hrs	27.2hrs

Note: Maximum speed and service ceiling varied widely with load and can differ when quoted in operating manuals, frequently the source of 'claimed' performance figures.

deep-penetration reconnaissance to carry out those searches with B-29s. The cover story was a plan by the United Nations to determine whether there were undiscovered lands and to assign territorial rights, but the real story was very different.

Operating out of Ladd Field, Fairbanks, Alaska, it would help establish the survey work necessary to set up a US military base at Thule on Greenland, but the purpose was far more important for mapping any islands which could be used as suitable places from which to recover strategic bombers after attacking targets in the Soviet Union. The US Navy was involved with several research vessels and information provided by the cameras carried by these B-29s supported surface and subsurface exploration. The part played by submarines in penetrating Soviet waters along its northern border is still classified today.

Variants of the B-29 were developed, especially the F-13A, which were extensively uprated for photographic work and for flights exceeding 30 hours in duration. In all, 118 F-13/F-13A variants were equipped with three K-17B, two K-22, and K-18 cameras, the type designation changing to FB-29J in 1948. These missions were supplemented with additional equipment for electronic intelligence (ELINT) flights from early 1947, beginning

with B-29 45-21812. Over time, other aircraft were involved, notably the RB-45C which did much work along and across the Chinese border, but it was the precedent set by these operations that attracted SAC to the B-36 for other types of reconnaissance.

After the communist coup in Prague during February 1948, the blockade of Berlin four months later, the detonation of the first Soviet atomic bomb in August 1949, and the attack on South Korea by communist forces in June 1950, that December President Truman authorised the first overflight of the Soviet Union with the B-47 specifically assigned to that task, but this was cancelled when the aircraft selected was destroyed in a fire at Eielson AFB, Alaska.

Operations envisaged with reconnaissance versions of the B-36 supported SAC requirements for attack profiles in the event of a major war with the USSR. Attacks from the continental United States (CONUS) would be made over the Arctic and information about Soviet defensive systems across the vast coastline of Siberia was largely unknown. B-17s and B-29s converted for reconnaissance (weather) duties had been probing the Arctic region, flying up and down the Soviet northern territories trying to light up defensive radars but there were none. The first overflight had taken place on May 10,

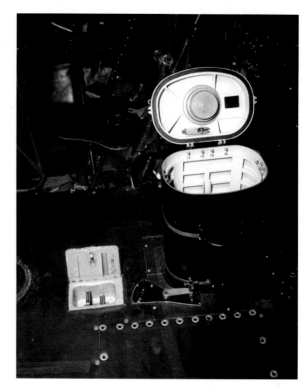

ABOVE: *An open MA-1 radiosonde dispenser chute, the equipment stack being in the intermediate frequency operator's station in the aft pressurised compartment. Don Pyeatt via Dennis Jenkins*

1948, when 1st Lieutenant Poe flew from Misawa Air Base, Japan, flying over the Kuril Islands, followed on March 10, 1950 with the first overflight of the Soviet Union to take pictures of the naval base at Vladivostok.

But SAC wanted flight profile simulations of attack routes from CONUS bases to Soviet targets for targeting nuclear weapons. This was different to the general intelligence information sought by the US Air Force through the RB-45 and the RB-47s and smaller aircraft such as the RF-80, RF-86, RF-100, and the navy's F2H-2P, initially known as SENSINT (Sensitive Intelligence), a code not to be confused with that name used by Westerners operating in Moscow engaged in human intel-gathering activities.

Responding quickly, the first reconnaissance version destined for SAC, RB-36D 44-92088, made its first flight on December 14, 1949. Piloted by George Davis and Francis Keen, that flight lasted seven hours and one minute. This aircraft was delivered to SAC ahead of the first B-36D bomber configuration, as were the next six reconnaissance versions of the D-series, albeit originally ordered as B-36Bs. The first arrived with SAC in June 1950. These aircraft were operated by the 28th SRS at Rapid City AFB, North Dakota, now Ellsworth AFB, and all 24 had been delivered by May 1951.

Early evaluation included a calibration of the cameras on a photo target comprising a set of white lines against a black background set up at a parking lot at Convair, where employees were asked not to leave their cars! Some of these test flights could be long. Fifteen hours into one such evaluation

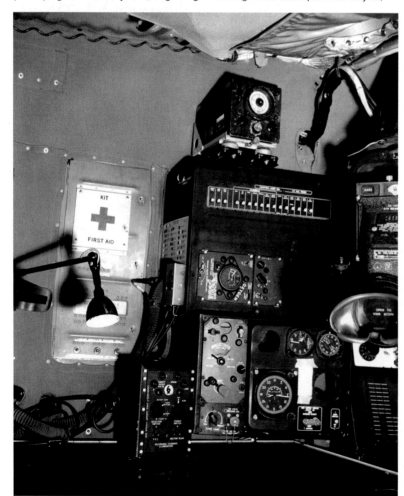

LEFT: *Control stations for the weather reconnaissance equipment. Don Pyeatt via Dennis Jenkins*

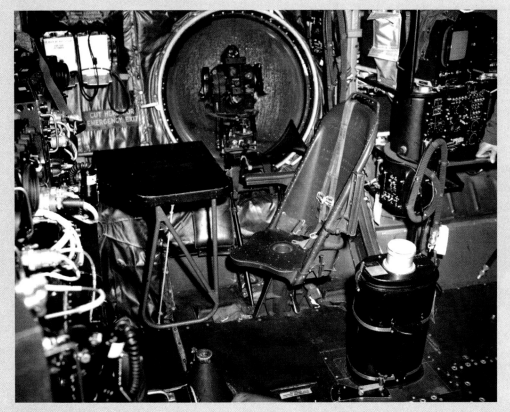

ABOVE: *The location of the radiosonde on the floor and at right, one of the many changes to the RB-36 variant. Don Pyeatt via Dennis Jenkins*

BELOW: *Built as one of the B-36A production lot, this RB-36E (44-92020) from the 28th SRW was one of the conversions with podded J47 engines and associated equipment. USAF*

flight, Beryl Erickson and Francis Keen were given a call to divert to Eglin AFB to participate in a synchronised air show with a 15 second window to appear at full throttle and all engines at maximum revs. As the only B-36 with jet pods, the air force wanted to impress. Streaking across the airfield and closely followed by two B-36Bs dropping a full load of 500lb (227kg) bombs in front of the grandstand, the RB-36D pulled up and made a steep climbing bank. No rehearsal and not even a day's work – back to the scheduled test profile, a further 32 hours in the air and a landing 47 hours 45 minutes after take-off.

The new capabilities of the reconnaissance version were demonstrated on January 16, 1951, when an RB-36D (44-92090) landed after a flight lasting exactly 51 hours 30 minutes. Flown by a Convair test flight crew, this flight was not that far beyond the duration of many operational flights, routine missions of more than 30 hours being considered normal. RB-36D 44-92088 spent its entire life flying test missions and was given the designation ERB-36D, the only one modified to carry the phenomenally complex Boston Camera.

Developed by Dr James Baker at Harvard University and officially designated K-42, it was built by Boston University's Optical Research Laboratory. It had a focal length of 240in (609.6cm) folded through a series of mirrors and was equipped with a lens with an f/8 stop and 1/400th of a second shutter speed. The K-42 weighed 6,500lb (2,948kg) and had a resolution of 28 lines/mm which allowed

it to show a golf ball from an altitude of 45,000ft (13,716m).

This is still the largest camera ever built and produced photographs on negatives 18 x 36in (45.72 x 91.44cm) from film stored on two 18in (45.7cm) wide reels. Spectacular in concept and highly impressive, the camera was tested for about a year from 1954 but serious problems with vibration produced a high percentage of smeared photographs, unusable for sensible intelligence purposes. It was removed from the ERB-36D and because of the amount of work required to restore the aircraft to operational use it was scrapped in 1955.

A product of the original order to adapt existing B-36B aircraft into reconnaissance versions, the next series to fly was the RB-36E, based on YB-36 42-13571 which was remodelled into the new role. The first production RB-36E (44-92024) took to the air on July 7, 1950, and was delivered to the 28th SRW at Rapid City AFB on July 28, the last of the 22 in this series being delivered on April 27, 1951.

The 36 RB-36F series were contracted under the same order of April 13, 1949 which launched the B-36D series. The first RB-36F took to the air on April 30, 1951, the last being delivered in December that year. The basic aircraft was similar to the B-36F, the reconnaissance equipment being the same as that applied to the RB-36D. It was on one of these aircraft that a pressure bulkhead failed causing a temporary altitude restriction.

The RB-36H was by far the most prolific of all reconnaissance variants, 73 aircraft of this series being produced after the contract was announced on September 5, 1951. The agreement had been reached the preceding year which provided serial numbers bearing the fiscal year 1950. As with the RB-36F, in this variant the airframe was identical to the B-36F while the reconnaissance package was unique to all variants modified into this role.

Goblins and Tom-Tom

In the search for capabilities extending its role, the giant B-36 was considered as a carrier for parasitic reconnaissance fighters while Convair tried to turn it into a cargo plane.

Operational use of the B-36 as a bomber, strategic asset and nuclear deterrent was extended to reconnaissance duties with significant modifications. In carrying out these flights over politically contested areas, many claims were made by air crew proud of their assignments and consistently effective in their duties. In reality, the B-36 played a secondary role in the acquisition of intelligence information through reconnaissance and area surveillance, the latter obtained through consistent monitoring of strategically important areas.

Most overflights were conducted by other aircraft, more than 80% carried out by the much faster RB-47s. With the advantage of aerial refuelling and height, these all-jet, camera-carrying spy planes provided valuable information

which helped decide target strategies and shape strategic war-fighting policy with conventional and nuclear weapons. The prerequisite for expanded activity came from intelligence itself, indicating that the Russians were constructing airfields in northern Siberia for Tupolev Tu-4 bombers, preparatory to crossing the Arctic Ocean and striking US and Canadian targets in North America.

Concern about the emergence of an over-the-Pole-threat was so acute that a special project was authorised by President Truman in the closing year of his second term as President. With the code name Project 52 AFR-18, it involved two specially modified B-47s from the 360th BW at MacDill AFB, Florida, for deep penetrations into Siberia using very different routes. The two aircraft took off on October 15, 1952, refuelling from two KC-97 tankers

before joining a racetrack pattern over the Chukchi Sea. The flight lasted almost eight hours and covered 800 miles (1,287km) inside Soviet airspace.

The separate intelligence-gathering requirements of SAC and the air force, together with the various US national intelligence services, added to a considerable database of detailed photographic and electronic information. But the intensity of overflights was great. Between July 1946 and December 1956, almost 200 military overflights took place, those before the first reconnaissance mission of May 10, 1948 conducted with general observation aircraft. These far outnumber the 24 U-2 missions conducted between July 1956 and May 1960.

Because of undetected Soviet agents and sympathisers living as normal

ABOVE: *The McDonnell XF-85 Goblin was a bold attempt to test the concept of a parasitic fighter/escort aircraft with a unique design influenced by some German experimental projects from World War Two. USAF*

ABOVE: *The Goblin was equipped with four, forward-firing guns in a configuration which also proposed air-to-air missiles for offensive armament. USAF*

American families in the United States, flight plans for these penetration missions were highly secret, the air crew only being told their destination when they had flown a routine training circuit of CONUS as they headed out to foreign parts from non-residential areas out of visual range. These clandestine destinations helped maintain secrecy from covert agents and LeMay was totally convinced that they were necessary on all B-36 flights as well. This has led to many urban myths, exaggerated by not a few seeking to dramatise the importance of their flights. But the reconnaissance missions conducted by the RB-36s were as vital as the role played by bomber variants and their highly professional crews.

Nevertheless, in support of the overall war-fighting strategy at SAC, the single largest overflight ever conducted was Operation Home Run, involving RB-47s flying 156 penetration flights from Thule AFB, Greenland between March, and May 1956. They flew to areas right along the Arctic seaboard of the USSR almost as far west as Murmansk and as far east as Provideniya, a coastline 3,666 miles (5,900km) in length. To reach the Siberian coast required a 1,900 mile (3,057km) flight just to get to Murmansk, the more easterly flights taking considerably longer heading in that direction.

Long before the requirement for penetration missions, the possibility of using large bombers to carry smaller combat aircraft with a dual role as escorts and reconnaissance assets attracted attention. Especially so with a new generation of aircraft emerging from design and into the flight test phase. On January 29, 1944, the

USAAF asked industry to examine the possibility of a parasitic fighter design for the B-29, the B-35, and the B-36. Nobody really knew how to do that and only one manufacturer provided a conceptual design.

On March 19, 1945, McDonnell proposed a small, egg-shaped aircraft with a triple vertical tail, short, swept-back stub wings and power provided by a 3,000lb (13,344kN) Westinghouse J34-WE-7 axial-flow turbojet engine. With a pressurised cockpit and an ejection seat, the XP-85 Goblin could carry four 0.50 calibre machine guns. On paper, McDonnell confidently projected a top speed of 648mph (1,042kph). The concept worked by way of a trapeze mounted beneath the belly of the bomber, extended for the Goblin to engage a latch on its nose with a hook at the bottom of the trapeze. Thus snagged, the trapeze would fold back up and the parasite would be secured beneath the fuselage of the carrier-plane.

Simple in concept, it was attractive and drew support from the air force, who on October 9, 1945, ordered two prototype XP-85s (46-523 and 46-524) together with a static test article. It also required the 24th production B-36, a B-series variant, and all subsequent aircraft of this type to be capable of carrying the Goblin. From that emerged an expanded capability which envisaged that some bombers would be capable of carrying up to three parasites without a bomb load, the idea being that formations of B-36s (the air force was still thinking World War Two style massed fleets of bombers) could be protected by fighter-carrying escort B-36s releasing swarms of such fighters to fend off attackers.

RIGHT: *The mated mock-up of the XP-85 with its trapeze design, although there would be subtle changes to this configuration. McDonnell*

All this was contingent on flight test results and plans were quickly made to buy 30 production Goblins, but conservatism and precautionary moves abandoned that plan for retaining just the two XP-85 prototypes to see how they operated on real flight trials. Only then would the production order proceed. The Goblin itself posed a lot of questions: designed for carriage on a trapeze, it did not require an undercarriage, only a retractable hook, but if it had to make an emergency descent for a landing, skids would allow safe touchdown.

By June 1946, a mock-up of the Goblin was put together at the St Louis factory and a B-29B-65-BA (44-84111) was assigned to modifications for the trapeze and preliminary flight trials. XP-85 46-524 was dropped in mid-air for a test run on August 2, 1948, and all went reasonably well, the vicissitudes of the Goblin notwithstanding, until the pilot, Ed Schoch approached for a hook-up, misjudged the closing rate, and rammed the underside of the trapeze smashing the canopy.

Schoch managed to land on the skids, but the Achilles heel of the concept was the return and hook-up phase, which successive tests proved was risky and fraught with potential catastrophe. Turbulence did nothing to ease the operation and four of the seven attempts resulted in pilots

having to break away and land on the skids. The second Goblin conducted a single captive flight on March 19, 1949, and the only free flight was carried out on April 8, 1949, which, although successful, did little to restore faith in the concept.

The programme was abandoned on October 24, 1949, and 46-523 was retired to the Air Force Museum, the second Goblin going to the SAC Museum. There was a legacy in the form of the existing mounting brackets for the trapeze which were retained on the first few B-36Bs of the many which the US Air Force had expected would

carry fighters designed to protect the vulnerable bombers all the way to their targets.

Ficon Flies

The concept of a parasitic fighter escort stuck and evolved quickly into the FICON (FIghter CONveyor) programme which succeeded the Goblin project. The XP-85 was believed to have been difficult to fly due to the unusual nature of its shape and the instability under airflow conditions set up by the carrier-plane. While the Goblin was clearly inappropriate for the carrier concept, it was possible that a slightly

ABOVE: *The RF-84F (49-2430) with a GRB-36 (49-2707) about to receive the Thunderflash with its anhedral horizontal tail surfaces. Convair*

larger and much more conventional aerodynamic design would be acceptable.

The Republic F-84E Thunderjet was selected and on January 19, 1951 Convair received authorisation to convert RB-36F 49-2707 for trials with this aircraft. This time, the B-36 itself would be the test carrier and a larger trapeze was designed to keep the F-84E clear of the worst turbulence from the big bomber. In this design, the fighter would insert a probe into a special boom funnel which would secure it at the nose at which point the trapeze boom would retract, raising the fighter into a saddle to secure it either side of the fuselage and lock it at three points. Under the designation GRB-36F (JRB-36F from 1955) bomb racks were replaced by the retractable cradle directly attached to the wing spar.

The FICON concept had the advantage of integrating two existing aircraft designs, both of which were capable of independent flight and landing, while the F-84E would have to be released for the B-36 to land safely. And that was the weak point in the system, urging the project engineer Ben Hohmann to push for explosive bolts which could jettison the parasite in the event that electrically operated separation devices failed. This was a move approved by Major Clarence E 'Bud' Anderson, selected to fly the F-84E (49-2115) in tests.

Initially, those proved difficult, with oscillations from the heavy turbulence beneath the GRB-36F and on one occasion the F-84E was unable to unlatch, the back-up emergency jettison coming into play to save both aircraft. Then it was discovered that the boom itself was too long and it was shortened, the nose hook on the parasite aircraft being moved to a position on top of the fuselage just forward of the cockpit.

RIGHT: *A schematic depiction of the trapeze and associated equipment for the air-deployment and recovery procedures involving the RF-84F Thunderflash. Convair*

This required a closer approach to the carrier-plane before hooking up, but the ensuing attachment was considered more rigid. It was tricky, the JRB-36F flying close to the stall speed of the F-84E.

During the initial test of the revised system the parasite approached the carrier, and all appeared well until the hook-up occurred followed immediately by a loud BANG! and the F-84E swung violently to the right, inducing the pilot to disconnect and fall away, a recovery procedure made tricky as Anderson had shut down the engine and was by now below the stall speed. In the 10,000ft (3,048m) remaining he managed to relight the engine and recover to land back at Carswell AFB. Unimpressed with the handling and the entire procedure, Anderson spoke openly about his opposition to the FICON concept, prompting the air force to introduce other pilots to share the tests.

By this time, the concept of fighter defence for big bombers was ebbing away, coincident with the introduction of the B-47 and the imminence of the B-52. If used in aggression it was reasoned that the nuanced value of escort aircraft would be irrelevant and the value of protection from various aircraft in a fleet of intruding bombers once again fell into disfavour. But reconnaissance missions were lone flights and an entirely different proposition: devoid of bombs, the cavernous bays on an RB-36 were available for a protective parasite.

In theory, a fast reconnaissance fighter could be carried by an RB-36 to the perimeter of hostile airspace, releasing the camera-carrying fighter to conduct a high-speed dash and return for a pick-up and withdrawal. For this duty, the air force chose the swept-wing RF-84F

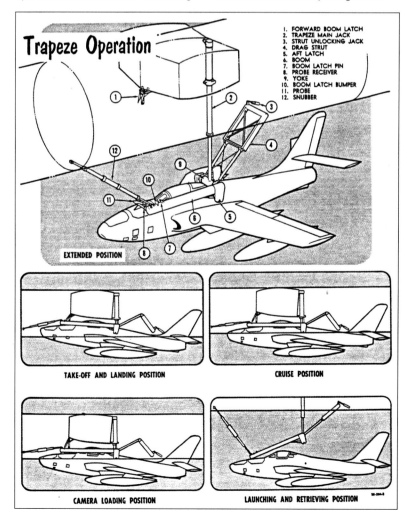

Trapeze Operation

1. FORWARD BOOM LATCH
2. TRAPEZE MAIN JACK
3. STRUT UNLOCKING JACK
4. DRAG STRUT
5. AFT LATCH
6. BOOM
7. BOOM LATCH PIN
8. PROBE RECEIVER
9. YOKE
10. BOOM LATCH BUMPER
11. PROBE
12. SNUBBER

EXTENDED POSITION

TAKE-OFF AND LANDING POSITION

CRUISE POSITION

CAMERA LOADING POSITION

LAUNCHING AND RETRIEVING POSITION

Thunderflash, specifically adapted for reconnaissance duty. The YF-84F (49-2430) was chosen for tests similar to those with the F-84E, except for the relocation of the horizontal tail which was canted down to clear the underside of the RB-36 during departure and approach. Early trials revealed a high level of flutter at the tail of the parasite, solved by re-profiling the remaining segments of the remodelled bomb bay doors.

By this time, the air force was getting excited about this extension of its capabilities and wanted to show off its new adaptation; there had been criticism of the B-36, that it was too slow and lumbering a platform to have relevance in the jet age. This was an ideal way to show that a relatively low-cost asset (the jet parasite) when carried to the border of a hostile state could do a valuable job made possible only by the availability of a carrier-plane to place it in harm's way and recover it with valuable intelligence information.

The air force revealed the FICON, as it existed at this time, during the National Aircraft Show in Dayton, Ohio, during August 1953. In a flurry of B-36 appearances, two flying directly in to the show from Japan and two more from the UK, the YF-84F and the JRB-36F performed several hook-ups. Other public demonstrations were conducted at Eglin and Carswell.

As 1954 began, Convair had a contract from the US Air Force for 10 RB-36Ds and 25 RF-84Fs, the carrier-plane modified according to Featherweight Configuration 3 with the new ECM equipment. But this was a reduction from the 30 RB-36s and the 75 RF-84s that the air force wanted. The converted aircraft received the designations GRB-36D III and RF-84K, the first carrier-plane taking to the air on July 28, 1954, piloted by Ray Fitzgerald and Fred B Perry.

Although testing on the carrier-plane was over by September 22, the

ABOVE: *Bomb bay two adapted the fixtures and fittings for the FICON programme with modified doors and closeout shields to improve airflow when mated to the RF-84F. Via Dennis Jenkins*

first RF-84K was not ready before December 17. But in the intervening period problems hit the programme and although a trapeze jack failed on the carrier-plane it did not interrupt delivery of the first aircraft to the air force in February 1955, followed in August by the first RF-84K.

The preferred operating procedure had the RF-84F take-off independently and join up with the carrier-plane, but it was also possible to carry the parasite into the air hung semi-buried in the under-fuselage, albeit displaying minimal ground clearance with its two underwing drop tanks requiring the rotation off the runway to be handled sensitively. Convair had to use ramps to jack up the GRB-36, but two pits were built at Fairchild AFB to accept the parasite, offering it up to the carrier-plane rolled in over the pit.

On a standard mission the carrier would release the parasite at a distance of 800 miles (1,287km) to 1,000 miles (1,609km) from the target, a nominal 2,810 miles (4,521km) from take-off. Specially sculpted doors (known as plug-and-clearance doors) enclosed the parasite in the converted bomb bay, and these closed after releasing the RF-84F. Following its planned penetration flight the parasite would return to the GRB-36D and return to base. The carrier-plane was fitted with an APX-29A IFF rendezvous set, and the bay had a catwalk area with hand holds and safety wires. With a 1,140 US gal (4,315 lit) supplementary fuel tank on the port side of the fuselage containing JP-4 jet fuel, the carrier-plane could refuel the parasite should that be necessary.

Training on the new configuration began at Convair in late 1955 during which 13 pilots from Fairchild AFB went through a rigorous familiarisation with the new concept, returning to their home base for more extensive, pre-operational training before assignment to classified missions. These included a wide range of potentially clandestine flights, some of them for night operations, re-rendezvous with the carrier-plane aided by a system of lights installed in the under-fuselage of the carrier plane. The GRB-36D went into operational service with the 99th SRW at Fairchild, operating RF-84Ks from the 91st SRS of the 71st SRW based at Great Falls AFB, Montana, and then at Larson AFB, Washington.

The pilots who flew a lot of clandestine operations were subject to special terms of constraint and

LEFT: *A GRB-36D (49-2696) carrying an RF-84F (51-1847) which has been uplifted. Via Dennis Jenkins*

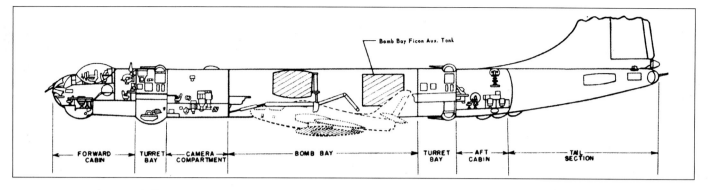

Bomb Bay Ficon Aux. Tank

FORWARD CABIN — TURRET BAY — CAMERA COMPARTMENT — BOMB BAY — TURRET BAY — AFT CABIN — TAIL SECTION

ABOVE: *The configuration of the GRB-36 with the parasite in the adapted bomb bay aft of the camera compartment.* Convair

RIGHT: *Jacks lift the aft end of the GRB-36 (49-2696) to receive the RF-84F which is moved into position beneath the fuselage.* Via Dennis Jenkins

BELOW: *In this view from inside the bomb bay, the RF-84F is retracted into a shoe with contains the upper part of the Thunderflash's fuselage.* Via Dennis Jenkins

secrecy. Undoubtedly, several penetrations into Soviet airspace were carried out, the GRB-36Ds staying in international airspace, releasing their parasitic snoopers to go about their own business. On several flights, the carrier-plane crew knew nothing of the sorties conducted, or of the targets selected for photo-reconnaissance,

but it is clear that these RF-84K flights gathered up electronic intelligence as well as photographic information, with some 'special' missions conducted in the brief interval between the start and finish of parasite operations.

Conceived in 1954, the Lockheed U-2 signalled a new era in spy plane operations and the FICON concept faded away. Quite quickly, the emphasis on reconnaissance departed to niched and highly specialised intelligence gathering missions with the A-12 from 1963 by the CIA and the SR-71 operated by the air force from 1966. But it had been the B-36 which had seen the most bizarre form of overflight espionage during a brief period in the mid-1950s on missions so important that there is largely a veil over them 70 years later.

From Tom-Tom to a Cargo Plane

There were advocates of carrier-plane parasites who refused to go away and who reverted to the air defence capability, ironically a successor to Goblin but using the ubiquitous line of F-84 aircraft. Promoted by ex-German scientist Dr Richard Vogt, and known as TOM-TOM, it began as a way of extending the range of bombers and reconnaissance aircraft by attaching free-floating fuel tanks articulated to the wing-tips of the aircraft to which they

were attached. With an aerofoil profile to allow them to provide lift and reduce drag, they could also increase their range and altitude by increasing the aspect ratio of the wing; range would be increased by the extra fuel, altitude achieved by the adaptation of the fixed wing planform, and weight removed by jettisoning them when empty.

These ideas were developed from wing-tip fuel tanks to parasitic escort fighters which could ride on their own wings while passively attached to a carrier-plane, their engines shut down. Advocates believed this free ride could dramatically extend the operational capability of the parasites and the Tom-Tom concept pressed by Vogt was a direct product of trials carried out in Nazi Germany during 1944 and early 1945. Post-war, preliminary tests had been conducted by the US Air Force using a Douglas C-47A and a Culver PQ-14B, with an attachment sufficiently flexible to allow three-degrees of freedom but riding on its own lift. The first attempt at coupling up in flight occurred on August 19, 1949, and it was not successful.

But this small-scale evaluation showed promise and, with the B-36 programme under way, the air force took the idea a step further, initiating a full-scale air-tow concept using a B-29 to tow a pair of F-84 fighters in Project TIP TOW. Republic modified two

LEFT: *The Tom Tom concept with wing-tip shoes for receiving the RF-84F in unmodified configuration for a fuel-free ride to free-flight after releasing close to photographic targets. USAF*

F-84D-1RE aircraft and designated them EF-84D with wing tips carrying flexible mountings to attach to suitably adapted wing tips of an EB-29A (44-62093). The risks were high and, despite some modest success, on April 24, 1953, all three aircraft plunged into Peconic Bay, Long Island, killing those on board after one of the two parasites flipped over and struck the B-29 wing.

Two RF-84F-5-REs (51-1848 and -1849) were modified to carry wingtip hook equipment and on May 8, 1954, the FICON JRB-36F test aircraft was assigned to what was named the Tom-Tom project. This time the entire coupling system design and manufacture was consigned to the Thiebolt Engineering Company and a fixed mock-up was attached to the wing of JRB-36F and an RF-84F logged some seven hours of proximity testing completed on September 30, 1954.

A retraction mechanism firmly clasped the parasite and made electrical and hydraulic connections to allow the fighter to shut down its engine.

Following the TIP TOW crash, tests were wound down. On November 2, 1955, the first aerial hook-up was accomplished with a fighter on the port wing and on September 26, 1956, the final hook-up resulted in violent oscillations that broke the connecting sleeve and the parasite fell away to land safely, as did the JRB-36F. The programme was cancelled and thus ended the dream of using parasitic free rides to augment the range of the escort fighter or to carry to enemy territory a fast reconnaissance system, superseded by much more efficient methods of extending range or obtaining vital intelligence information.

Back in the early development stages of the B-36 programme, the AAF

wanted a heavy-lift cargo freighter to support wartime operations and on December 31, 1942, it ordered a prototype (43-52436) designated XC-99. It was not the only interested customer. News of the B-36 programme reached Pan American and it saw in the giant aircraft a potential flying boat through a derivative akin to that it had negotiated with Boeing to transform the unsuccessful XB-15 into the 314 Clipper utilised on its profitable routes from the West Coast to the Philippines.

The Pan American flying boat adapted from Convair's B-36 would, said the airline, be marketed as its Super Clipper and carry 204 passengers and up to 15,000lb (6,804kg) of freight. Lavish interior décor and a staircase at each end of the spacious fuselage would serve gourmet meals to both upper and lower decks occupied by premium fee-paying passengers and

BELOW: *The inboard profile of the XC-99 cargo-carrier which failed to convince US Air Force officials of its value for a production contract. Convair*

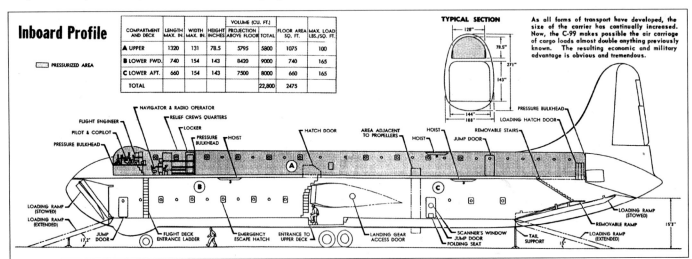

Inboard Profile

▨ PRESSURIZED AREA

COMPARTMENT AND DECK	LENGTH MAX. IN.	WIDTH MAX. IN.	HEIGHT INCHES	VOLUME (CU. FT.) PROJECTION ABOVE FLOOR	VOLUME (CU. FT.) TOTAL	FLOOR AREA SQ. FT.	MAX. LOAD LBS./SQ. FT.
A UPPER	1320	131	78.5	5795	5800	1075	100
B LOWER FWD.	740	154	143	8420	9000	740	165
C LOWER AFT.	660	154	143	7500	8000	660	165
TOTAL					22,800	2475	

TYPICAL SECTION

As all forms of transport have developed, the size of the carrier has continually increased. Now, the C-99 makes possible the air carriage of cargo loads almost double anything previously known. The resulting economic and military advantage is obvious and tremendous.

RIGHT: *Convair Model 37, designed from the initial XC-99 concept into landplane and flying boat configurations for Pan American. Convair*

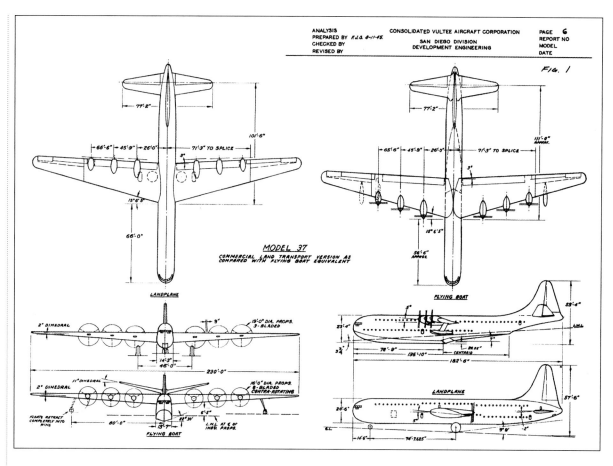

ANALYSIS PREPARED BY *F.J.S. 8-11-45.*
CHECKED BY
REVISED BY

CONSOLIDATED VULTEE AIRCRAFT CORPORATION
SAN DIEGO DIVISION
DEVELOPMENT ENGINEERING

PAGE **6**
REPORT NO
MODEL
DATE

FIG. 1

MODEL 37
COMMERCIAL LAND TRANSPORT VERSION AS
COMPARED WITH FLYING BOAT EQUIVALENT

LANDPLANE

FLYING BOAT

FLYING BOAT

LANDPLANE

facilities to equal the best hotels in the world. In February 1945 Pan American ordered 15, six-turboprop engined Super Clipper flying boats and Convair, seeing a marketing opportunity, proposed a landplane alternative.

Although a fitting prescient for the wide-body, dual-deck airliners of the future, it was too big for the passenger market of the early post-war years and an unprecedented expansion of both airfields and a surplus aircraft market bridged the gap from piston-power to the age of the commercial jet transport. Flying boats were out, the Atlantic market would control the expansion of the early peacetime years until

turboprop landplanes served the regional needs of local airlines and the early Boeing and Douglas jet airliners opened up intercontinental travel.

As for the US Air Force, the XC-99 cargo carrier made its first flight on November 24, 1947, and would conduct many record-breaking runs between the United States and continental Europe carrying up to 60,000lb (27,216kg) of freight, some flights of up to 12,000 miles (19,308km). While demonstrating to the air force the outstanding lift capacity and performance of this cargo carrier, it spent most of its time ferrying engines and supplies around from the United

States to destinations in Japan and Southeast Asia.

While the air force liked it, corrosion and stress fatigue foretold its demise and it was retired out of the service in 1957 to oblivion, now resting at the AMARC facility, Tucson, Arizona, awaiting funds and willingness to restore it to a permanent display at the National Museum of the US Air Force (NMUSAF), Wright-Patterson AFB. It is only marginally better remembered by the four surviving B-36 aircraft on public display: B-36H 51-13730 at Castle Air Museum, Castle AFB, Atwater, California; B-36J 52-2217 at the Strategic Air Command and Aerospace Museum, Ashland, Nebraska; B-36J 52-2220 at the NMUSAF; and B-36J 52-2827 at the Pima Air and Space Museum, Davis-Monthan AFB, Tucson, Arizona - the last built.

Over time the B-36 will retain its place in history and in the annals of Strategic Air Command. Although difficult to fly and subject to numerous technical challenges and not a few failures, only 32 of the 385 aircraft built were lost to accidents. A credible record for its time, well above average and a fitting tribute not only to the design, engineering, and operation of one of the most extraordinary aircraft operated by the US Air Force in its long history but to the aircrews who served in it and the ground crews who kept it flying through one of the most challenging periods of the Cold War.

BELOW: *The Convair XC-99 flying near La Jolla, California. USAF*

Flying the B-36

It took a combination of individual skills and teamwork to fly the B-36,
"like sitting on your veranda and flying the house around," said one pilot.
Three of those who flew and crewed the Peacemaker describe their experiences.

Francis H. Potter, Colonel USAF Ret

"I was a 1st lieutenant, with about 1,500 flying hours, recently returned from a tour flying cargo aircraft on the Berlin Airlift. I was assigned to the 9th BWH, flying primarily B-29s. We were to transition to the B-36s as they became available from the factory at Ft Worth, Texas. We soon had three or four of these wonderful, modern, new aircraft, with crews formed to man them. Since we had pilots with more experience than I, my assignment was as a crew co-pilot. My crew was somewhat down the line on the check-out list, so we spent our free time ogling this beauty, and talking about it with those already in the programme.

During this time, the air force set up a ground school for prospective aircrews at Rapid City AFB, South Dakota, which I attended in the fall of 1949. I believe it was the first training school where crew members came from other bases to a central location to receive training. This proved an effective operation and was used from then on. The B-47 had such a school in Florida, the B-52 in California, etc. It proved a most efficient way of training.

My first flight, a round robin which kept us airborne for 30 hours, came on January 18, 1950. There were several pilots on board, all scheduled to receive training. My instrument check was due which gave me priority to be aboard. Can you imagine, taking an instrument check on your first flight in a new aircraft, one of this enormity and complexity? The newest and most sophisticated bomber in the world at the time! I don't remember much about it, except the check pilot was satisfied. My white instrument card was renewed.

Although the new bomber was interesting and fun to fly, it had one rather naughty problem that gave the maintenance men a real fit. It wouldn't hold its gas. That's right. We were plagued with gas leaks. I recall seeing several leaks seeping from the wing sections and at the same time, drips in the bomb bay. Burning hi-octane aviation gasoline, this was not a problem to ignore. It didn't take too long to become evident that this was a problem that could not be fixed by on-base band-aids, it would require something more drastic. So, after having them for less than a year our B-36s were returned to the company to fix their leak problems.

"Here is other trivia data that really impressed all who qualified to fly this bird. The wing was more than seven feet (2.1m) thick at the root. A person could climb into the wing and work his way outboard of the centre engine. The 19ft (5.79m), square tipped props were geared to turn approximately one half engine speed to keep them sub-sonic, which gave that unforgettable throbbing. Each aircraft used 336 sparkplugs, a big portion of which required replacing after each mission.

"My next association with the B-36 came in late summer 1954. I was

BELOW: *Eielson AFB, Alaska, in the harsh conditions of winter, February 1959, where aircraft were serviced in extreme cold conditions.*
Via Dennis Jenkins

ABOVE: *A B-36B (44-92038) accepted in December 1948 and operated by the 9th BS, 7th BW at Carswell AFB but converted to B-36D at San Diego before being lost in a fire.*
Via Dennis Jenkins

BELOW RIGHT: *Four B-36Bs approaching Lake Michigan on July 3, 1949, as they head for Chicago.*
Vis Dennis Jenkins

assigned to the 92nd BWH at Fairchild AFB, Washington. The 92nd had three squadrons, flying the D and J models. Shortly after I checked in, the wing departed for a 90 day deployment to the island of Guam. By now I had 3,200 hours of four engine flying time. I had been checked out as an aircraft commander, bomb commander, and instructor pilot in the B-29s. So, I was put into the programme to be an aircraft commander. The wing had left a couple aircraft along with three or four instructor pilots at the home station. After seven instructional flights and

two ferry flights, I was a checked-out aircraft commander, and soon after upgraded to instructor status.

"I still remember the first time my crew and I took off with me at the controls, and no instructor personnel on board. Although I felt entirely comfortable with my check out and the many simulator hours had taught me emergency procedures, there is still something special about that first mission in the left seat. Without an instructor you feel all alone and have that somewhat 'now or never' attitude. As we lifted off and climbed into the clouds (there were always clouds at Fairchild) I recall thinking, 'I hope I can get this big mamma back on the ground all in one piece'.

"Many interesting occurrences happened during the nearly 1,200 hours I was to spend in this aircraft. One, that earned my crew the coveted 'SAC Crew of the Month' award for January 1956 occurred in late 1955. We were flying a routine bombing navigational training

mission. We had been out quite a few hours and, due to a turbo compressor problem, were operating with less than full power on two engines. We were on a night navigation training leg when the gunners reported the exhaust shroud around one of the engines had failed. This let the very hot exhaust gas shoot back through the engine nacelle and was considered very much a fire hazard. We shut the engine down which solved that problem. In less than 10 minutes the gunner reported the same problem on another engine. We shut it down. So, with two of six shut down and two with partial power, we headed home. We started the jets, which were normally shut down during cruise, and used them to help hold altitude sufficient to get over the mountains. Arriving at Fairchild AFB, we had low visibility and a ceiling of 500-600ft (152-183m). But, true to their advertising, the GCA unit brought us in through the clouds and mist perfectly lined up with the runway.

After landing, a servo did not close, so the nose wheel steering would not work. Just another mission, but one we didn't need to repeat.

"Many other remembrances come to mind. The first time I landed on packed snow was interesting. It was on a deployment to Eielson AFB, at Fairbanks, Alaska. We were briefed we'd be landing on an inch or more of 'packed snow'. We were also advised that if we were aligned properly at touch down, it would make the landing much more pleasant. Our landing, as well as the others, all went well. For this deployment, we had 'snow' tyres installed. These were tyres with what appeared to be steel wool moulded into the tyre. If you ran your hand along the tread, you'd get a hundred scratches. They seemed to do a lot of good. In the other temperature extreme, I remember the 'greenhouse' effect you got in that big glass cockpit, when on the ground in the hot sun. There was no air-conditioning, just a small fan which just moved the hot air. The sun would beat in through the glass and the temperature would soar. Many times, I would be completely soaked with sweat before take-off.

"We were required to fire our guns each training quarter. To do this we usually went several hundred miles over the ocean. When we were in position and had no ships visible on radar, we'd give the command to fire! What a racket they made. It seemed that if several turrets fired in the same direction, you could feel the recoil through the aircraft controls. To keep from over-heating the gun barrels, the gunners were to practice shooting in short bursts,

then take so much cooling time before continuing to fire. The extended turrets were into the slipstream which caused added drag, requiring more power to hold air speed.

"And then there were the super-secret 'sniffer missions'. This was during the Cold War and Russia as well as we were doing tests using atomic explosives. When our intelligence got wind of a proposed Russian test, we would fly out near Attu, on the Alaskan chain and hold for hours. All such missions would run 20 hours plus, so we could stay at our assigned location for many hours. Our aircraft were equipped with air pumps and a filter system which would extract particles from the air. Upon return these special filters would

be analysed and the 'smart' people could tell the approximate yield of the detonation. While in the air we had no way of knowing if we were getting a 'hot' filter or not. If the detonation was delayed, we'd go out the next night. One time, I believe we went out three times before the Ruskies actually let it go.

"We also ran missions giving the Tactical Air Command a chance to show their expertise in defence of the ADIZ (Air Defense Identification Zone). An exercise would be scheduled. The defenders would know it was scheduled sometime during a period of several days. "Sometimes we would go single ship, sometimes several aircraft together. I recall going north, to near

ABOVE: *Wooden spade brooms used by ground personnel to clear snow and ice in perilous conditions and without safety gear.*
Via Dennis Jenkins

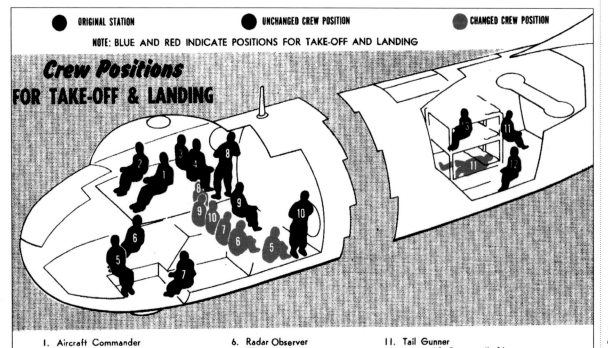

LEFT: *Relative crew positions for take-off and landing were rarely adhered to rigorously but the crew manual displays the required locations.*
Convair

1. Aircraft Commander
2. Pilot
3. Second Engineer
4. First Engineer
5. Navigator
6. Radar Observer
7. Observer
8. Second Radio Operator
9. First Radio Operator
10. Copilot
11. Tail Gunner
12. Lower Aft Scanner (Left)
13. Lower Aft Scanner (Right)

RIGHT: *Evacuation routes for crew members in the event of an emergency exit. Convair*

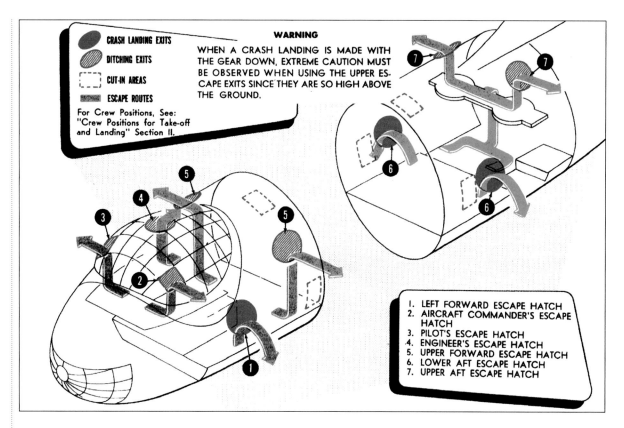

WARNING

WHEN A CRASH LANDING IS MADE WITH THE GEAR DOWN, EXTREME CAUTION MUST BE OBSERVED WHEN USING THE UPPER ESCAPE EXITS SINCE THEY ARE SO HIGH ABOVE THE GROUND.

- CRASH LANDING EXITS
- DITCHING EXITS
- CUT-IN AREAS
- ESCAPE ROUTES

For Crew Positions, See: "Crew Positions for Take-off and Landing" Section II.

1. LEFT FORWARD ESCAPE HATCH
2. AIRCRAFT COMMANDER'S ESCAPE HATCH
3. PILOT'S ESCAPE HATCH
4. ENGINEER'S ESCAPE HATCH
5. UPPER FORWARD ESCAPE HATCH
6. LOWER AFT ESCAPE HATCH
7. UPPER AFT ESCAPE HATCH

Alaska, then heading toward Hawaii, then turning east to enter the ADIZ around mid-to-northern California. If there were 10 bombers in the exercise, there could be 10 different flight paths. Or you could have one bomber follow another, 10-15 minutes later.

We bombers would be at our optimum altitude and airspeed watching for the fighters. I recall seeing the fighters, probably F-89's, come in for a head on attack. They'd pass us by with a closure speed of around 850mph (1,367kph). That was usually the only pass they

could make. By the time they turned around, we were fairly hard to catch. After the fighters with afterburners came into use, that would change. We were also permitted to intercept their radio frequencies, except for emergency channels and give false instructions. We often disrupted their games using this medium, anything to confuse them!

"I had one especially exciting take off from Eielson AFB at Fairbanks, Alaska. At that time, their runway ran through some fairly dense woods. The trees had been cleared perhaps 200-300

yards (183-274m) on each side. I had a young third-pilot on board and was letting him make the take-off. He was a husky individual, just like a football player. As we started our acceleration down the runway and the nose started to lighten for lift off, the aircraft wanted to go to the right. I told the young pilot to 'give it some left rudder'. I could see no change, the nose still wanted to go right. I repeated my instructions and looked at his legs at the same time. I could see him straining so hard on the left rudder, his leg was actually

1. FORWARD ENTRANCE HATCH
2. CATWALK ENTRANCE HATCH (TO BOMB BAY)
3. LOWER AFT ESCAPE HATCH
4. AFT CABIN HATCH
5. LOWER AFT ESCAPE HATCH
6. COMMUNICATION TUBE DOOR
7. LEFT FORWARD ESCAPE HATCH

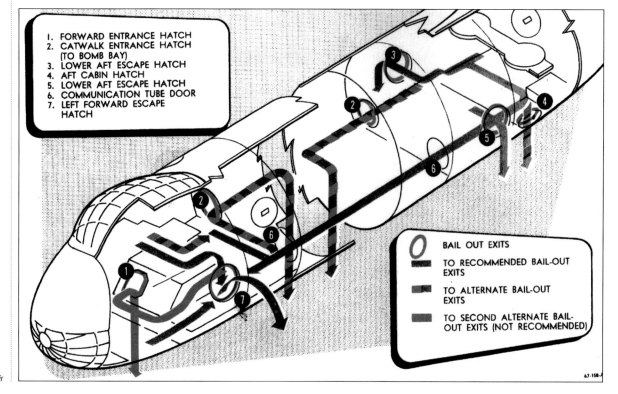

BAIL OUT EXITS
- TO RECOMMENDED BAIL-OUT EXITS
- TO ALTERNATE BAIL-OUT EXITS
- TO SECOND ALTERNATE BAIL-OUT EXITS (NOT RECOMMENDED)

67-158-

RIGHT: *Primary and secondary bale-out routes with the locations of exit hatches for both pressurised areas. Convair*

quivering. I tried applying left rudder too, but it would not budge. By this time, we were a good distance down the runway with the nose getting lighter all the time. So, I called to abort the take-off.

I pushed the nose firmly onto the runway and reversed all six recips [reciprocating engines] while still at take-off power. I didn't think I had time to bring them to idle, reverse, then increase power. My first co-pilot was watching the take-off from between the pilots' seats. He beat me to retarding the throttles on the overhead panel that controlled the four jets. We were able to stop, stay on the runway and not blow any tyres, but talk about the noise! By reversing all six engines at take-off power, that baby really screamed, bounced, and bucked! The noise and vibrations in that cold air were horrendous. As we taxied back to the parking area, all the workers in the nearby buildings were out watching to see what made all that noise. The maintenance people found that the electrically controlled hydraulic

servo that locked the huge rudder while on the ground had failed to release, preventing the rudder from moving. There was no way the aircrew could check this on the ground, since the rudder pedal moved only the servo trim tab, which along with the slip-stream caused the rudder to move. I felt I never needed to repeat that exercise.

"In August 1956, my crew was picked to give a short, four hour orientation flight to 18 AF ROTC cadets. We took off, climbed to a medium altitude, and showed them the sights of the area. Grand Coulee Dam, the Columbia River and the large lake behind the dam, Mt Rainier, etc. They all seemed to enjoy the flight; none got airsick. Years later, I was approached at different times by two individuals who told me they were one of the cadets who participated and remembered that flight! Just shows what a small world it really is.

"In April 1956, our wing again deployed to Guam for our 90 day rotation. We had my crew of 15 aboard, along with some 20-25 ground crew

ABOVE: *Convair photographer Frank Kleinwechter at Goose Bay, Labrador, with a B-36F (49-2680) in the background.* Via Dennis Jenkins

members. In those days we did not have the support of cargo aircraft, so carried most of our freight and support personnel with us. We departed Fairchild at full gross weight, flew west to the coast and set up our flight at 5,000ft (1,524m). We held that altitude for perhaps eight to 10 hours, then being lighter, we climbed to perhaps 12,000ft (3,657m). After some time, we'd increase altitude again. We stair-stepped all the way to Guam.

"After 30 flying hours we arrived at Guam. When we extended the landing gear lever for landing, the left main gear would not unlock. This required one of the flight engineers to go into the wing, go to the wheel well and pull the manual 'unlock' handle. After doing this

LEFT: *Delivered in December 1948, B-36B 44-92041 displays the lower aft escape hatch as a circular disc below the national insignia.* Via Dennis Jenkins

BELOW: *This B-36B presents an appealing view across a cloud covered sky, its orange Arctic recognition colour a distinctive identification.* Via Dennis Jenkins

the gear came down and locked. We landed without further incident. Ninety some-odd days later, we returned to Fairchild. The wing commander, Colonel Roland Campbell decided he would return aboard my aircraft. This was somewhat an honour and let us be the first aircraft to depart Guam and the first to arrive back home. This time, they led us to the base operations area, usually reserved for transient and special aircraft. After we parked, a red carpet was rolled out along the commander's exit path. Course, we crew members told our wives it was rolled out for us!

"My crew and I were picked to 'get rid' of one of the (Mk 17) practice bombs we had on base. It was the same dimensions as the real thing, but instead of having explosives, was filled with concrete to give the same weight. Its purpose was to give loading crews experience in handling and loading that large a weapon. So, one of them was loaded onto our aircraft. To 'get rid' of it, our flight path took us 400 miles (644km) out over the Pacific Ocean.

It was well after sundown when we got to the designated spot. We cleared the area with radar, and seeing nothing on the water, dropped that 41,400lb (18,598kg) hunk of steel and concrete. We had talked about the possible reaction the aircraft would display, losing that much weight so quickly. I remember we retarded the throttles slightly but felt no great bounce. I often wondered how deep into the floor of the ocean that 'bomb' went.

"Other memories are also vivid. We had a lot of instrument flying here at Fairchild, so we were on a first name acquaintance (almost) with the GCA operators. During the winter months nearly all landings were actual GCA's and during the good weather we practiced the procedure. It was hard to get the B-36 to settle down on a specific heading and hold it without wavering a degree or two to each side. It seemed like you just orbited around the heading you desired, sloshing back and forth, until you were on the ground.

"The nose of this aircraft was a series of windows, each held in its place in a metal framework. When in moist, warm air, we could get some terrific St Elmo's fire. It would snap and jump across the windows and run up and down the wings. Just a bluish ribbon of light dancing all over, back across the top of the wing, etc. It was fascinating to watch. It was so bright at times you could read by it. I am not aware of it

ever doing any damage and when you were used to it, it was fun. Newer crew members sometimes didn't agree. Some were quite apprehensive.

"The only time I ever got even slightly airsick was in July 1955. The Air Force Academy at Colorado Springs, Colorado, was to be opened and dedicated soon. There was to be a three-ship B-36 flyover. My crew and another were picked to fly down and make some practice runs to get a feel for the area. One aircraft was provided by each of three different wings. We met the other two aircraft in the academy area, joined into a three-ship formation and made quite a number of low altitude passes over the grounds.

Seems I flew for an hour or so, then the other crew took over. I went downstairs to sit out the remaining time. The air was extremely turbulent and being at low altitude for such a long time, the air inside the aircraft was quite warm. This warm, somewhat foul air, along with the constant bouncing gave me a minor case of air-sickness. When the time came a few days later for the actual dedication and flyover, my crew was not chosen. I did not have to make the trip a second time and didn't mind a bit.

"In 1956, like all things, the era of this magnificent monster was to end for us. My wing was scheduled to transfer into the newer eight engine, all jet B-52s. What a change that was going to be.

Instead of lumbering along at 200 mph (322kph), we'd do our cruise at .77 Mach, about three quarters the speed of sound. Instead of returning to our home station and taking nearly an hour to get on the ground, we could accomplish the same thing in about 10 minutes. So, no-one felt we'd rather hang onto the old 36s. As 1956 progressed, we started flying the big old birds to re-assignment bases.

"On March 25, 1956, my crew was assigned to fly the last B-36 aircraft (a J model) away from Fairchild. We delivered it to the Bomb Wing at Biggs AFB, El Paso, Texas. Fittingly it was another cloudy, rainy day. After take-off, about mid-morning and while still below the clouds we made a circular

ABOVE: *Flight crew for the last B-36J (52-2827) in Featherweight Configuration III, first delivered in August 1954, pose for a publicity picture.* USAF

BELOW: *Accepted by the US Air Force in December 1948, B-36B 44-92037 was upgraded to a B-36D Featherweight Configuration II and operated by the 42nd BW at Loring AFB. Via Dennis Jenkins*

RIGHT: *Visiting RAF Lakenheath, England, in January 1951, this B-36D (49-2658) made an impression on British plane-spotters and the general public!* Via Dennis Jenkins

trip around the base. What a change! Instead of seeing some 35-40 big birds roosting on the ground, all we could see was wet concrete. Sad!

"Since retiring I have heard a time or two of an operational B-36 being flown at altitudes I find difficult to believe. Certainly, I'm not the last nor best expert, but when I see figures of 50,000ft (15,240m) plus and at one time better than 55,000ft (16,764m) I'm curious. I don't know what they were fuelling their birds with, but ours, using hi-octane av/gas gasped and struggled to get to and maintain 45,000ft (13,860m). All ten throttles were at or near the firewall to maintain that altitude. In rechecking the Dash 1, both the D1 and the D2 oxygen pressure demand regulators were rated as adequate for altitudes only to 43,000ft (13,106m). From 43,000-45,000ft (13,106-13,716m) they were rated as 'marginal'.

"A caution states that at 50,000ft (15,240m), (when unpressurised) no more than two to three minutes of consciousness can be anticipated using either regulator. Hopefully, this would give enough time to initiate

a descent. And wasn't the figure of 55,000ft (16,764m) what the altitude chamber people used to give as the atmospheric pressure point where a person's blood will boil when un-pressurised. I never heard of any crew in our outfit being so daring or foolhardy.

"So, the big bird really earned its nickname, The Peacekeeper. It never dropped a bomb nor fired its guns in anger. It was truly the most effective deterrent during the long Cold War with the communist countries. Its retirement truly signalled the end of a great era. I would never wish to punch the delete or diminish button on any of the great, fond, and vivid memories I have. It was really the era of the 'big bombers'!"

Bob Miller, Tail Gunner, Corporal USAF Ret

"I was in the USAF 1952-56 through Lowry B-29 gunnery thence to Carswell AFB training for B-36 as tail gunner. Eventually formed with other transfers as a member of a combat-ready crew and shipped to Limestone (Loring AFB, Maine)

"After the final phase-out of B-29s out of Korea and everywhere else

(no match for MIG-15s) a further diminished number of us found ourselves at Carswell AFB, Fort Worth, Texas - the home of the famed B-36. Essentially, we were then processed into a cram-course on 20mm cannon, remote-controlled turret mechanics, newer pedestal and yoke-sights, AN/APG-32 gun-laying radar, and a dry school on 'enemy' target recognition. Some of us, myself included, also took a hands-on black-box orientation to radar fundamentals, waveguides, magnetrons, dish di-poles, and CRT image recognition of range, azimuth, and elevation. The training seemed rushed and left me and my pals with huge ring-binders of scanner's and gunner's S.O.P. and a later tome of '*Emergency Procedures for the B-36 Heavy Bomber*'.

"In about five Texas months, my most vivid recollections are the very hot summer, car trips to the flesh-pots of Dallas for a weekend, ice frozen beers on the road between Fort Worth and Dallas (although I was still, legally, under age) – and a vain attempt to join a sorority dance and other disappointments! Nevertheless,

BELOW: *A B-36F (49-2652) assigned to the 7th BG at Carswell AFB displays the type's distinctive nose-down attitude.* Via Dennis Jenkins

'senior gunner' (Tony Giamanco) was just recently made a 'buck sergeant' and the rest of us 'aft people' were all corporals: John Pfor from Nebraska, Rich Kunzman from Iowa, and K Y Landsdale from Kentucky, plus me from Oregon. I wondered how these old veterans like Mailander trusted any of us!

"There were six bunks in the aft compartment of all the models I rode, also an electric stove with four burners where we presumably could cook ham and eggs but we seldom, if ever did that, even on long missions of more than 30 hours. Inflight 'box lunches' were not all bad, except for the ubiquitous 'Purple Plums in Syrup', and the vitamin fortified chocolate bar. Advancement for combat-ready crews was more rapid than in the rest of the air force, (we were told) our AC, pilots

LEFT: *Defensive tail armament gets an inspection while technicians get to work on the piston-engines using bespoke access gantries.*
Via Dennis Jenkins

by mid-August 1953 we had completed the B-36 gunnery school orientation flights on that huge aircraft and after just eight hours total 'inflight instruction' we were introduced to the 12 members of our student crew which to me was fairly frightening.

"My AC (aircraft commander) looked to be at least 50 years old (he was actually in his early 40s). Captain Mailander, who was a veteran pilot who 'Flew the Hump' in World War Two smiled at me and then asked, 'how many days ago was it that you left your momma'? I think I just grimaced for about 30 seconds, and then said slowly 'My momma's been dead for quite a few years, Sir'. After that introduction Captain, (later Major) Mailander and I never exchanged a word beyond required intercom talk for as long as he was my AC.

"Other members of my crew were more congenial, but there was a natural rift or distance from the officers up front who were all career air force and the aft compartment who were, essentially, raw, young recruits. Our pilot was Captain Roy Kirkland, a veteran of World War Two and Korea. He was a quiet man, very professional and (I learned later) looking to a day when he could retire back to his farm in Louisiana. Other officers were 1st Lieutenant Ford, bombardier, Captain Martin, navigator, (a graduate of Annapolis, I never found out how he made it to SAC) and also a second lieutenant West Pointer, as 'Third Pilot' whose name I can't recall. Later, Maj Mailander was kicked upstairs to Omaha, I think, replaced by Captain (Later) Major Black Barney, a much more outgoing, cheery, happy leader, whom we all (I think) got to respect and love.

"Among the enlisted crew we had a staff sergeant radio operator and a World War Two B-17 master sergeant/first radio operator and another master sergeant as second flight engineer. After that, our

and radar/nav/bombardiers all gained heavier metal within the first 18 months after passable flight safety records and good bombing scores.

"In early August 1953 we had some small wings awarded to us which looked like miniature bombardier wings and were given a three week furlough home along with new orders to go to Limestone, Maine. My trip home was aided by a C-47 hop to San Francisco, from whence I took a Greyhound Bus to Portland, Oregon. My reporting date to Limestone, ME was September 5 and accomplished by a long train ticket with transfers in Chicago, New York, and Hartford, and, finally Presque Isle, Maine, where I was met by a blue bus and a sergeant who knew my name.

"Four days without a bunk or a change of underwear, and it was already cold and wet when I processed into a long line of new people at Limestone. My attitude changed when I finally was driven to my assigned quarters, a brand new barracks but it was brick, with large windows, hardwood floors, rooms with bunks much wider and deeper than anything I had seen before, beautiful sanitary latrines (comparatively speaking), a day room with a television, a gymnasium, and even special mess halls and open hours for flight crews. Maybe this wasn't going to be so bad.

"First hand events that I experienced, between September 1953 and January 17, 1956, when I left the service, included almost regular in flight malfunctions of our reciprocating (R-4360) engines. After the first couple of feathering events preceded by smoke and flame, or just a decision to shut down a misbehaving engine running

too rich - we all just took such events in our stride most of the time. One day en route to England in 1954 we feathered the No.3 (inboard starboard engine) just as we left the east coast of Greenland. We were probably cruising at about 25,000ft (7,620m) or 28,000ft (8,534m) flying into night with daylight behind us.

"Before long, after a nap, I replaced Johnny Pfor as left scanner. He told me something strange about losing altitude and to be sure to wake him if necessary. I wasn't sure what he was talking about, but I learned more after listening to intercom chatter for a few minutes. Our flight engineer(s) and the pilots were apparently discussing options about carburettor icing, or wing icing and losing power across the board. Within about ten minutes after taking over for

BELOW: In August 1953, SAC sent 20 B-36s from the 92nd Bomb Wing to Kadena Air Force Base in Japan on Operation Big Stick. USAF

Johnny Pfor we were instructed to locate our water survival suits and be ready to review ditching procedures. I don't recall any exact sequence of events after that message, but I do know that we all got very alert in the aft compartment. We all were doing exactly what was asked, without a curse or complaint but I felt horrible because I knew that we (after many missions) had still never reviewed or practiced deployment of our 20-man life raft and we all knew that our water survival suits were absolute bullshit, prone to be less than watertight, to tearing, and hard to get into in the cramped aft compartment.

"The end of this episode was after about four hours of fighting with the engines and losing, then gaining, then losing altitude, we got to within radio distance of Keflavik, Iceland and then at no higher than 1,800ft (549m) we were able to start the jets, notice a change

in outside temperature and decide to neither ditch nor attempt an emergency landing in Iceland but to climb to a reasonable altitude and, after taking inventory of our remaining fuel, proceed to Upper Heyford, UK.

"I don't have a clue about the particulars of how our aircraft 'healed itself' but our flight engineers and pilots wrote it up as a victory of 'out thinking the malfunctions'. I don't know if this episode was ever reported or recorded in flight safety reports, but I do know that it was, by far, NOT the most serious event concerned with malfunctioning engines or icing that other crews from Loring AFB had experienced. One of my roommates, John Yost, of Lawrence Kansas, gave us a vivid account of a No.6 engine literally burning the nacelle off its engine mounts and the whole unit, (prop blades, engine, and all) falling off into the ocean.

"I think I became disillusioned with the whole notion of the B-36 during my last months of service. I had learned to put up with the rather frequent gun jamming incidents where we almost never were able to expend our 20mm ammunition beyond a few bursts. No matter how many times we critiqued our ammo belts, or torqued our electric breech loaders, some of our guns jammed or just quit, again and again. This was not only my crew, but it was also an epidemic in the 69th, 70th, and 75th. Such malfunctioning lost emphasis, or actually went unreported, simply because after about May of 1955 we were flying H and J (reconnaissance) models, with either no guns, or just tail guns, and we almost never carried ammo or engaged in shooting rounds into the ocean.

"Even after becoming an 'elite' crew or elevated to the exalted role as an

ABOVE: A family visiting day at Eglin AFB, Florida, on October 12, 1955, provided opportunity to inspect a B-36H (50-1086) and two 24,000lb (10,890kg) bombs. Via Dennis Jenkins

BELOW: The clean wings of the B-36B are displayed here by 44-92028. USAF

ABOVE: *With the application of Featherweight Configuration III measures, this B-36J (52-2824) shows skin tone changes between the magnesium and aluminium fuselage panels. Via Dennis Jenkins*

BELOW: *An Oregon ANG Lockheed F-94B (51-5450) escorts a B-36D (44-92033) across cloud-filled skies. Via Dennis Jenkins*

'instructor' I began to sense that the mighty B-36 was probably no more than a political victory of the air force that got way out of hand. That our vaunted capabilities were never fully revealed, for good reasons: we were a long range bomber when our major load was gas and thus loaded, we could and did fly for 40 hours and nearly 10,000 miles (16,090km). But with a bomb load or the featured nuke of that day our radius was much, much shorter.

"In the Loring enlisted barracks, it dawned on several of us that we might just be part of a yet undisclosed scam that had fooled enough people

(including enemies) for just long enough to build a new generation of effective and new (jet) aircraft that were actually lethal, that were actually capable. I guess I began to think that this deception was my reason for being, rather than the notion that the B-36 was anything like a survivable war machine. Logically our aircraft was just a 'Peacemaker- threat' that I had to stand behind regardless of the facts that I became aware of. I never expressed this feeling to anyone outside my own circle of friends. We were all far too obedient, too willing to execute our duties as well as possible. Quite frankly, I think we also were afraid to voice our

reservations. We were also reasonably certain that those 'profile' missions we had been flying would more than likely never happen.

But what I did know was that we seldom even reached a true airspeed above 287mph (462kph), that headwinds like the jet stream from west to east made a simple flight from Loring to Fairchild ten hours or more going direct. So, we made it look good by going out of our way and 'bombing' Boulder Dam and attacking Mount Hood en route.

"We aft cabin people learned that even the jets could get us into a sprint of no more than 402mph (647kph) or a bit faster with J series or 'featherweights'. Then, on one mission in late summer 1955, we simulated a broad 'attack' on the northeast coast of the USA. I think all our squadrons were involved, perhaps 30 aircraft. Somewhere in the west Atlantic maybe 300 miles (483km) from Boston we hit a headwind of (probably) 138mph (222kph). Our ground speed was reported by the navigator to be 'less than 86mph (138kph)'. We were swarmed by East Coast Air Defense Command (ADC), noticeably by F-89 Scorpions from Otis AFB and a number of swept-wing types. To get to my point, we began to know just how obsolete we were when, at the debriefing of this exercise, it was noted that ALL, as in EVERY 45th Bomb Wing B-36, was 'shot down' multiple times, some as many as 20 times according to gun-camera results.

"I kept noticing that SAC was now far more interested in B-47 capabilities and deployments, that air to air refuelling

and speed were factors. Several -47s began remaining parked on our tarmac for extended days. In late 1955, we were greeted with a visit by the prototype B-52, still with the tandem cockpit. Looking at that thing convinced me that they (SAC, Curtis LeMay et al) were probably done with us and with a huge sigh of relief that we had kept the myth of the B-36 alive...just barely long enough to be useful. I also began to realise at age 22, just how ignorant I was, and I was determined to leave the service and go to college."

Ken Wallis, Wing Commander RAF

"I was a senior specialist armament officer in the RAF on exchange posting to Strategic Air Command, Offutt AFB between 1956 and 1958. As one of the four pilots on board, it was the giant RB-36H of which I have the strongest memories. I would go down to Carswell AFB, Fort Worth, Texas, and be kitted out with clothing intended to ensure survival at the North Pole if necessary. An early morning start would be made on the pre-flight inspection of the huge aircraft involving some climbing in the wings, etc. By the time the inspection was finished it was as though one had done a day's work, but it was time to climb aboard and start the very long flight.

"When taxiing, the aircraft was steered by a large hand wheel on the port side of the cockpit. Take-off would be at a very heavy weight with the six piston and four jet engines at full power. The take-off run would go on and on until a very gentle detachment from the ground and a very slow climb. At an altitude of 10,000-15,000ft (3,048-4,572m) the engines would be shut down and the umbrella-like seals in the jet air intakes would be adjusted to allow just enough air in to keep the engines wind-milling to prevent icing up. The long cruise to the simulated target would then start, passing north over the USA and Canada

and heading for the region of the North Pole.

"During the flight two pilots would take four-hour shifts at the controls before handing over to the other two pilots. Most of the time we would be on autopilot but at intervals we would revert to manual to re-trim the aircraft as the immense fuel load was consumed. In fact, for about the first 10 hours the attitude would be distinctly nose-up to maintain height at such a weight. The cockpit area and forward part of the aircraft was pressurised as was an area aft accessed via a small, pressurised tunnel 84 ft (25.6m) long. A small trolley allowed a crew member to lie flat on his back, but such was the aircraft's pitch angle for the first 10 hours of the 33 hour flight that a small handbrake down the right side of the trolley was needed to prevent an overshoot at the other end! Small windows in the tunnel allowed us to see the atomic bomb we always had on board – just in case war broke out

during the flight and orders came to divert to a real target. There was always an A-bomb on board.

"After the four-hour stint of flying, much of it in darkness, we would look forward to a little sleep in a hammock, but the sounds of cabin pressure changes, the note of the piston engines and general noise prevented anything other than fitful rest. We could, however, heat up ready prepared meals. Trouble with one or two of the piston engines was not uncommon but we always seemed to have enough power. As we approached the target the jet engines would be started and we would climb to 45,000ft (13,700m) for a simulated bombing run followed by a turn to starboard from where we would head north of Sweden and turn for England and a landing at Burtonwood. While ground crew performed the odd engine change and other work, I sometimes had the opportunity to nip home for a day or two!"

ABOVE: *One of four surviving examples preserved for posterity, Convair B-36 52-2220 is on display at the National Museum of the US Air Force at Wright-Patterson AFB. NMUSAF*

BELOW: *Miss Featherweight, B-36D 50-1086, brought to Configuration III standard and seen here over Mountain Home, Arkansas. Via Dennis Jenkins*